CONVERSATIONS
WITH
MY
FATHER

Also by Herb Gardner

A PIECE OF THE ACTION (NOVEL)

A THOUSAND CLOWNS (PLAY)

THE GOODBYE PEOPLE (PLAY)

WHO IS HARRY KELLERMAN AND WHY IS HE SAYING
THOSE TERRIBLE THINGS ABOUT ME? (SCREENPLAY)

THIEVES (PLAY)

I'M NOT RAPPAPORT (PLAY)

CONVERSATIONS
WITH
MY
FATHER

A PLAY BY
HERB GARDNER

A CORNELIA & MICHAEL BESSIE BOOK

PANTHEON BOOKS
NEW YORK

Grateful acknowledgment is made to the following for
permission to reprint previously published material:

CCP/Belwin, Inc.: Excerpts from "Santa Claus Is Coming to Town" by Fred J. Coots and Haven Gillespie. Copyright © 1934 and renewed 1962 by EMI Feist Catalog Inc. World Print Rights Controlled and Administered by CCP/Belwin, Inc. Excerpts from "Rum and Coca-Cola" by Morey Amsterdam, Paul Baron, Al Stillman, Jeri Sullavan. Copyright © 1944, 1956 and renewed 1972 by EMI Feist Catalog Inc. World Print Rights Controlled and Administered by CCP/Belwin, Inc. ● *Music Sales Corporation*: Excerpts from "Rumania, Rumania" by Aaron Lebedeff and Sholom Secunda. Copyright © 1945 (Renewed) by Music Sales Corporation (ASCAP). Excerpts from "In Odessa" by Aaron Lebedeff. Copyright © 1945 (Renewed) by Music Sales Corporation (ASCAP). International Copyright Secured. All Rights Reserved. Reprinted by Permission.

Library of Congress Cataloging-in-Publication Data

Gardner, Herb, 1934–
Conversations with my father : a play by Herb Gardner.
p.   cm.
ISBN 0-679-42405-9 (hardcover)
ISBN 0-679-74766-4 (paperback)
1. Fathers and sons—Drama. I. Title.
PS3513.A6333C65   1993
812'.54—dc20   92-50781

Book design by Jan Melchior

Manufactured in the United States of America
First Edition   9 8 7 6 5 4 3 2 1

For Barbara
and our fathers,
and for Jake and Rafferty
and our many
conversations to come.

FOREWORD

BY PETE HAMILL

The curtain goes up and suddenly we are in a saloon burnished with memories of New York past.

There is a wonderfully baroque jukebox and small tables and framed photographs of Benny Leonard and Barney Ross. Over the bar there's a giant moose head and a photograph of an ebullient F.D.R. American flags are everywhere. And a Yiddish song is playing: "Rumania, Rumania, Rumania . . . Geven amol a land a zise, a sheyne . . ."

We are suddenly in the world of Herb Gardner's luminous play, *Conversations With My Father* at the Royale, and we have been transported back to the New York that all of us have left behind. This is a play about a father and his sons, about the nature of being Jewish, about survival and disaster. But it's not at all narrow; by being specific, it's also universal. As a result, this layered, beautifully crafted play is about all those fathers who came to New York from terrible places, and all the sons who had to learn the sometimes dark and dreadful lessons about becoming Americans.

"Here's what we got going for us, kid," says Eddie Goldberg (played brilliantly by Judd Hirsch) to his two-year-old son, Charlie, who sits mute in a stroller. Eddie drops a nickel in the jukebox. "We got America."

He plays Paul Whiteman's version of "America the Beautiful," but this moment isn't hokey; it's ironical. Particularly as Eddie Goldberg talks to the child about his dream of moving from Canal Street to the dubious glories of Uptown:

"Now there's only two ways a Jew *gets* Uptown; wanna get outa here, kid, you gotta *punch* your way out or *think* your way out. You're Jewish, you gotta be smarter than everybody else; or cuter or faster or funnier. Or tougher. Because basically, they want to kill you; this is true maybe thirty, thirty-five hundred years now and is not likely to change next Tuesday. It's not they don't want you in Moscow, or Kiev, or Lodz, or Jersey City: it's the earth, they don't want you on the *earth* is the problem; so the trick is to become necessary. If they need you they don't kill you. Naturally, they're gonna hate you for needing you, but that beats they don't need you and they kill you, got it?" To which, in a moment, the Yiddish actor Zaretsky (who does a twelve-minute version of *The Dybbuk*) looks up from his newspaper and says: "Itzik, the only Jew in this room being persecuted is two years old."

That line gets a big laugh, and the play is full of laughter. Eddie is funny; his wife tells jokes; and irony suffuses the narrative. The play is a classic example of the way the funniest men are also the most serious.

This is not a tract about anti-Semitism; it's an entertainment, a drama of wit and intelligence that gets to your head by way of the belly. Eddie teaches his son to go to the body in street fights; Gardner does the same.

At one point, Eddie gives his two-year-old son the basic advice for survival in America and uses a sentence that chilled me: "Don't take shit from nobody." That was also the basic advice given to me in Brooklyn a half-century ago by my Irish-immigrant father. The same exact phrase. My father, who also had F.D.R. on the kitchen wall, would have loved Eddie Goldberg's saloon. And Eddie Goldberg too—even after he changed his name to Ross, in honor of the welterweight fighter and opponent of Jimmy McLarnin.

And as an Irish immigrant, he'd have understood the issues of the play. Like the drama in the theater next door—Brian Friel's *Dancing at Lughnasa*—Gardner's play is also about language: words, names, the lost language of Old Country myths. Long before the Jews surrendered Yiddish for English, the Irish language was slain by the Brits. The Irish Anglicized their names too. And every child of the Irish diaspora will understand what happens when Goldberg becomes Ross; Itzik becomes Eddie; his wife, Gusta, becomes Gloria. In the end, you are what you are. And even while cursing God, Eddie remains triumphantly Jewish.

Gardner's own father ran a saloon down by the old Police Headquarters on Centre Street, and the place, the emotions and many of the events are autobiographical. "But it's a collage," he said. "Some of my father, parts of two uncles . . ." Gardner is fifty-seven and grew up in Brooklyn; he remembers clearly the mini-pogrom that hit New York on election night in 1944, when the children of the American Right roamed the neighborhoods in search of Jews, whom they blamed for the war. "That happened," he said. "I was there."

Those events figure in the play. But they are not used to attack the idea of America; they are part of a larger affirmation. In this, his greatest play, Herb Gardner reminds us once again of the truth of Faulkner's line, that we love in spite of, not because.

Conversations With My Father was originally presented by the Seattle Repertory Theatre in April 1991.

The play was subsequently presented by James Walsh at the Royale Theatre in New York City on March 28, 1992. The cast was:

CHARLIE	*Tony Shalhoub*
JOSH	*Tony Gillan*
EDDIE	*Judd Hirsch*
GUSTA	*Gordana Rashovich*
ZARETSKY	*David Margulies*
YOUNG JOEY	*Jason Biggs*
HANNAH DI BLINDEH	*Marilyn Sokol*
NICK	*William Biff McGuire*
FINNEY THE BOOK	*Peter Gerety*
JIMMY SCALSO	*John Procaccino*
BLUE	*Richard E. Council*
YOUNG CHARLIE	*David Krumholtz*
JOEY	*Tony Gillan*

Directed by Daniel Sullivan
Setting by Tony Walton
Costumes by Robert Wojewodski
Lighting by Pat Collins

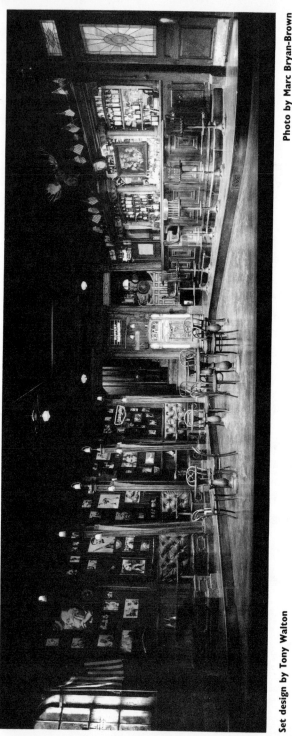

Set design by Tony Walton

Photo by Marc Bryan-Brown

CHARACTERS

CHARLIE

JOSH

EDDIE

GUSTA

ZARETSKY

JOEY, age 10

HANNAH DI BLINDEH

NICK

FINNEY THE BOOK

JIMMY SCALSO

BLUE

CHARLIE, age 11–13

JOEY, age 17

SCENE

*The Homeland Tavern—also known as Eddie Gold-
berg's Golden Door Tavern, The Flamingo Lounge, and
The Twin-Forties Café—on Canal Street, near Broadway, in Lower Manhattan.*

ACT I: Scene 1: June 25, 1976, early evening.

        Scene 2: July 4, 1936, early morning.

ACT II: Scene 1: July 3, 1944, early morning.

        Scene 2: About seven that evening.

        Scene 3: August 8, 1945, early morning.

        Scene 4: October 15, 1965, early morning.

        Scene 5: About eight weeks later, early
               morning.

        Scene 6: June 25, 1976, early evening.

ACT
ONE

Scene: *The interior of The Homeland Tavern on Canal Street near Broadway in Lower Manhattan, June 25, 1976. Although the place is obviously very old, some attempt had been made at one time to give it an Old Tavern style in addition. The original patterned-tin ceiling is there, the pillared walls, the scarred oak bar, the leaded-glass cabinets, the smoked mirror behind the bar, the high-backed wooden booths with their cracked leather seats, the battered and lumbering ceiling fans; but someone has tried to go Old one better here, a kind of Ye Olde Tavern look—a large, dusty Moose head has been placed above the mirror, its huge eyes staring into the room; an imitation antique Revolutionary War musket and powder horn hang on the wall over one of the booths, and over three others are a long-handled fake-copper frying pan, a commander's sword in a rusty scabbard, and a cheaply framed reproduction of "Washington Crossing the Delaware"; a large copy of the Declaration of Independence, with an imitation-parchment-scroll effect and a legend at the bottom saying "A Gift for You from Daitch's Beer," hangs on the back wall next to the pay phone, its text covered with phone numbers; a battle-scarred Old Glory print is tacked up over the yellow "Golden Door" of the entrance and a dozen copies of old oil lamps have been placed about the room with naked light bulbs stuck in them. But the genuinely old stuff is in dis-*

repair—absent panes in the glass panels, missing slats in the booths, gaps in the ceiling design, blades gone from the fans, moth-holes in the Moose-hide, dents in the pillars, the thick heating and water pipes acned by age and too many paint jobs—and the fake old stuff is just too clearly fake and second hand, so the final effect of the place is inescapably shabby. Somehow, though, there is still something warm, colorful, and neighbor-hood-friendly about the place; you'd want to hang around in it.

The bar runs along the left wall and the four booths run along the right, a few tables and chairs at center. The entrance is down left at the end of the bar, and on the wall behind the bar is a very large but not very good oil painting of four men playing poker and smoking cigars, one of them wearing a green eyeshade. Dozens of photographs of Boxers and Performers—the ones of Benny Leonard, Barney Ross, and Eddie Cantor are autographed—have been taped up around the mirror, as has the December 6, 1933, front page of "The New York Times" heralding the end of Prohibition; a large photo of Franklin D. Roosevelt, a cigarette holder clenched in his broad smile, hangs in a fancy frame over the cash register. Against the wall up center is a glowing red, yellow, and orange Wurlitzer Jukebox, Model 800, a beauty; to its left a door with a small circular window opens into the tiny bar-kitchen, and to its right a stairway leads up to the door of the Apartment over the bar where a family once lived.

At Rise: *Before the curtain goes up we hear the zesty, full-spirited voice of Aaron Lebedeff, backed by a wailing Klezmer Band, singing the beginning of an old Yiddish Music Hall song called "Rumania, Rumania"; an invitation to the joys of food, wine, romance, friendship, dancing, and more food. The song speaks of Rumania but it could be telling us about Odessa, Budapest, Warsaw, Lodz, Brody, the places of an older and better world that may never have existed but certainly should have.*

Lebedeff's Voice:
  "Rumania, Rumania, Rumania . . .
  Geven amol a land a zise, a sheyne,
  Ah, Rumania, Rumania, Rumania,
  Geven amol a land a zise, a fayne,
  Dort tsu voyen iz a fargenign,
  Vos dos harts glust kentsu krign,
  A Mamaligele, a Pastramile, a Karnatsele,
  Un a glezele vayn, aaaaaaaah . . . !"

(Lebedeff's Voice and the bouncing Klezmer Band continue as the curtain goes up and we see that the Music is coming from the Jukebox; its pulsing colors and the glow from the open Apartment door at the top of the stairs are the only real light in the bar at first. It is early evening, June 25, 1976; no one onstage, the upended chairs on the tables and the dim, dust-filled light tell us that the place has been closed for a while. The Music continues in the empty bar for a few moments.)

Lebedeff's Voice:
"Ay, in Rumania iz doch git,
Fun kayn dayges veyst men nit,
Vayn trinkt men iberal—
M'farbayst mit Kashtoval.
Hey, digi digi dam, digi digi digi dam . . ."

(A sudden rattle of keys in the entrance door and Charlie, early forties, casually dressed, enters briskly, crosses immediately to the stairs leading to the Apartment door, shouts up.)

Charlie *(trying to be heard above the Music)*: Josh! *(Opens Jukebox, turns off the Music, tries again.)* Josh!

Josh's Voice: Yeah?

Charlie: It's five-thirty. *(He shifts his keys from hand to hand, glancing about the bar, waiting for Josh; he clearly doesn't want to stay in the place any longer than he has to. He looks up at the Moose for a moment, then raises his hand in farewell.)* Well, Morris . . . goodbye and good luck.

(Josh, about twenty, appears in the Apartment doorway carrying an old folded Baby-Stroller, an antique samovar, some faded documents, a few dusty framed photographs.)

Josh: Who're you talking to, Dad?

Charlie: Morris. Morris the Moose. We haven't had a really good talk since I was twelve. Find some things you want?

Josh *(coming down stairs)*: Great stuff, Dad, great stuff up there. History, history. Grandma's closet, just the *closet*, it was like her own Smith*sonian* in there. *(Putting objects on table.)* You sure you don't want *any* of this? *(Opens Stroller, places it near bar.)* Look at this; perfect.

Charlie: Seems a little small for me, Josh. *(Reaches briskly behind bar for bottle of cold Russian vodka, knowing exactly where to find it, fills shot-glass.)*

Josh: Dad, believe me—some of the stuff upstairs, you really ought to take a look before I pack it up. Some extraordinary *things*, Dad—wonderful brown photographs full of people looking like *us*—some great old books, Russian, Yiddish—

Charlie *(briskly)*: It's all yours, kid. Whatever you can fit in your place. And anything down here; including Morris. Only the basic fixtures are included in the sale.

Josh *(not listening, absorbed in documents)*: Perfect, this is perfect, one of Grandpa's bar signs—*(reads from faded posterboard:)* "V.J. Day Special, the Atomic Cocktail, One Dollar, If the First Blast Don't Get You, the Fallout Will."

Charlie *(impatiently, checking watch, pointing up-stairs)*: Josh, it's getting late; pick what you want and let's go.

Josh *(reads from old document)*: "Declaration of Intention to Become a Citizen" . . . *Your* Grandpa, listen . . . "I, Solomon Leib Goldberg, hereby renounce my allegiance to the Czar of All the Russias, and declare my intention to—"

Charlie *(cutting him off)*: Got the station wagon right out front; pack it up, let's move.

Josh: I don't get it; only a month since Grandma died, why does the place have to be sold so fast?

Charlie: Leave a bar closed too long it loses its value. Customers drift away. That's how it works. Deal's almost set. *(Points upstairs.)* Come on, Josh, let's—

Josh: I don't get it, I just don't get it . . . *(Going up stairs.)* What difference would another *week* make? What's the hurry, what's the *hurry* here, man . . . ? *(He exits into Apartment. Charlie sits at bar; then looks up at Moose.)*

Charlie: He wants to know what's the hurry here, Morris.

(Silence for a moment, Charlie lost in thought; the Jukebox glowing brighter as we hear the sudden sound

of a full Chorus and Marching Band doing a thunder-
ous rendition of "Columbia, the Gem of the Ocean.")

Chorus and Band *(from Jukebox):*
   "Three cheers for the red, white and blue,
   Three cheers for the red, white and blue,
   The Army and Navy forever,
   Three cheers for the red, white and blue . . ."

(All stage lights, one section after the other, coming up
full now in strict cadence to the trumpets, drums and
Chorus: the many fake oil lamps, the overheads, the
bar-lights, the dawn-light from the street, all coming
up in tempo to reveal an image of rampant patriotism
only dimly perceived in earlier shadow—red, white and
blue crepe bunting hung across the full length of the
bar-mirror and on the back of each booth, and several
dozen small American flags on gold-painted sticks
placed everywhere about the room; the trumpets build-
ing, the ceiling fans spinning, as Eddie Goldberg, a
man in his early forties who moves like an ex-boxer,
bursts out of the Kitchen, a swath of bunting across his
shoulders, a batch of foot-high flags in one hand and
an individual flag in the other, waving them all to the
Music. July Fourth, 1936, and Eddie Goldberg have
arrived suddenly and uninvited—Charlie turning
slowly from the bar to watch him. Eddie wears a fine
white shirt, black bow-tie, sharp black pants and no-
ticeably polished shoes—an outfit better suited to an
Uptown cocktail lounge than to this Canal Street gin-
mill. He parks the batch of flags on a nearby table,
drapes the bunting with a grand flourish across the

Stroller, sticks the individual flag onto the hood—all these movements in strict time to the powerful March Music that continues to blare out of the Jukebox, his spirits rising with the soaring finale of the record, circling the Stroller once and finishing with a fancy salute to the Kid within, kneeling next to the Stroller as the record comes to a trumpet-blasting, cymbal-crashing end.)

Chorus and Band *(continued)*:
"When borne by the red, white and blue,
When borne by the red, white and blue,
Thy banners make tyranny tremble,
When borne by the red, white and blue!"

Eddie *(he points to the Moose)*: Moose. See? See the nice Moose? Moose, that's an easy one. An "M" at the beginning, "MMMM," and then "OOOO"; Moose. Mmmmooooose. See the pretty Moose? Just look at the Moose. Moose. *(He waits. Silence from the Stroller.)* Forget the Moose. We'll wait on the Moose. "Duckie." Hey, how about "duckie"? You had "duckie" last Saturday, you had it down cold. "Duckie." *(Reaches under Stroller, takes out wooden duck, presents duck.)* Here ya go, here ya go; duckie. *Here's* the duckie. Look at that duckie; helluva duckie, hah? Hah? *(Hides the duck behind his back.)* Where's the duckie? You want the duckie? Ask me for the duckie. Say "duckie." *(Silence for a moment; he leans against the bar.)* You lost it. You lost "duckie." You had it and you lost it. Now we're losin' what we *had*, we're goin' *back*wards, Charlie. *(Starts to pace in front of bar.)* Kid, you're gonna be two; we gotta get movin' here. Goddamn *two*, kid. I mean, your brother Joey—your age—we had a goddamn conver*sationalist* in there! *(Silence for a moment.)* Charlie, Charlie, you got any idea how much heartache you're givin' us with this issue, with this goddamn vow of *silence* here? Six words in two years and now *gornisht*, not even a "Mama" or a "Papa." *(Grabs the batch of flags, starts placing one on each table about the room; quietly, controlling himself:)* Frankly, I'm concerned about your mother. Granted, the woman is not exactly a hundred percent in the Brains Department her*self*, also a little on the wacky side, also she don't hear a goddamn word anybody says so why should you want to talk to her in the first place—nevertheless, on this issue, my heart goes out to the woman. She got a kid who don't do shit. She goes to Rutgers Square every morning with the other mothers, they sit on the long bench there—in every stroller, right down the line, we got talkin', we got singin', we got tricks; in *your* stroller we got *gornisht*. We got a kid who don't make an *effort*, a boy who don't *extend* himself. *(Leaning down close to Stroller.)* That's the *trouble* with you, you don't *extend* yourself. You never *did*. You don't *now*, you never *did*, and you never *will*. *(Suddenly, urgently, whispering:)* Come on, kid, gimme something, what's it *to* ya? I open for business in an hour, every morning the regulars come in, you *stare* at them; I tell 'em you're sick, I cover for you. It's July Fourth, a special occasion, be an American, make an effort. *(Grabs the duck off the bar, leans down to the Stroller with it.)* Come on: "duckie," just a "duckie," one "duckie" would be a Mitzvah . . . *(Silence from the*

Stroller; then the beginnings of a sound, barely audible at first; Eddie leans forward, smiling hopefully.) What's that? What . . . ? *(The sound grows louder, but there is no discernible word, and finally what we hear quite clearly is pure baby-babble, something like "ba-bap, ba-bap, ba-bap . . .")* Oh, shut up. Just *shut* up, will ya! If that's how you're gonna talk, then shut ya goddamn *trap!*

(Eddie turns sharply and throws the wooden duck violently across the room—it smashes against the farthest down right booth, barely missing Charlie, who has been seated in the booth, watching. Charlie turns, startled, as the pieces of the duck clatter to the floor. Eddie strides angrily over to the bar and then behind it, turning his back to the Stroller, starts to clean glasses from the sink and slap them onto a shelf as the baby-babble continues.)

Eddie *(shouting)*: The conversation is *over,* kid!

(The baby-babble stops abruptly. Silence for a moment.)

Charlie *(to Audience; calmly, cordially)*: Duck Number Sixteen; other casualties this year include four torn Teddy bears and a twisted metal frog. *(Rising from booth, moving down towards us.)* "Gornisht"—in case it wasn't clear to you—means "nothing." "Gornisht *with* gornisht" being less than nothing. The only thing less than that is "bupkes," which is beans, and less than that is "bupkes mit beblach," which is beans with more beans. In Yiddish, the only thing less than nothing is the existence of something so worthless that the presence of nothing becomes more obvious. Which brings me to the story of my life . . . *(Shrugs, smiling.)* Sorry; I can't resist a straight-line, even one of my own. I just—I hear them coming. I am often criticized for this. Oh, but they are everywhere and always irresistible: there are people who are straight-lines—both my ex-wives, for example, and all of my accountants—days, sometimes entire years, whole cities like Newark and Cleveland—"What did you do in Newark last weekend? I dreamt of Cleveland"—and some lifetimes, whole lifetimes like my father's, are set-ups for punch-lines. *(Moving towards Stroller.)* That's me in the stroller there and, as you can hear, I *did* finally learn to talk—last year I even started using the word "duck" without bursting into tears—*(We hear the sudden sound of the Kid crying; he leans down to Stroller, whispers gently.)* Don't worry, kid . . . in just a few years they'll be telling you you talk too much.

Eddie *(shouting)*: Gloria! *(Remains with his back to Stroller, continues briskly cleaning glasses.)* Gloria, the kid! Change the kid! *(The Kid is instantly quieter, comforted by the sound of his father's voice even though he's shouting.)* Gloria, the kid! Time to change him! *(Then, louder:)* For another kid! *(Turns towards stairway.)* Gloria, why don't you *answer* me?!

Gusta's Voice *(from upstairs, a strong Russian accent)*: Because I only been Gloria two and a half weeks . . . and I was Gusta for thirty-eight years; I'm waiting to recognize.

Eddie: I thought you liked the name.

Gusta's Voice: I liked it till I heard it hollered. Meanwhile, your wife, Gloria, she's got a rusty sink to clean.

Eddie: Hey, what about the *kid* here? I gotta get the bar open!

Gusta's Voice *(graciously)*: A shaynim dank, mit eyn toches ken men nit zayn oyf tsvey simches.

Charlie *(to Audience)*: Roughly, that's "Thank you, but with one rear-end I can't go to two parties."

Eddie: English! English! Say it in *English*, for Chrissakes!

Gusta's Voice: You can't say it in English, Eddie, it don't do the job.

Charlie: She's right, of course, English don't do the job. Sure, you can say "Rise and shine!," but is that as good as "Shlof gicher, me darf der kishen," which means "Sleep faster, we need your pillow"? Does "You can't take it with you" serve the moment better than "Tachtrich macht me on keshenes," which means "They don't put pockets in shrouds"? Can there be a greater scoundrel than a paskudnyak, a more screwed-up life than one that is ongepatshket? Why go into battle with a punch, a jab, a sock and a swing when you could be armed with a klop, a frosk, a zetz and a chamalia? Can poor, undernourished English turn an answer into a question, a proposition into a conclusion, a sigh into an opera? No. No, it just don't do the job, Pop. *(Eddie flips a switch, lighting up the freshly painted entrance to the bar.)* Behold . . . the Golden Door—*(taking in the bar with a sweep of his hand)*—and here, "Eddie Goldberg's Golden Door Tavern" . . . formerly "Cap'n Ed's Place," "The Café Edward," "Eduardo's Cantina," and "Frisco Eddie's Famous Bar and Grill"; living above it are Gloria and Eddie, formerly Gusta and Itzik, their sons Charlie and Joey, formerly Chaim and Jussel—*(a sweep of his hand up towards the Apartment doorway as Zaretsky enters)* and our boarder, Professor Anton Zaretsky—*(No matter how quietly or subtly, it is impossible for this old actor to come into a room without making an entrance—this same theatrical glow is true of his departures—proceeding purposefully down the stairway to the bar now, carrying his seventy years like an award, his unseasonably long, felt-collared coat draped capelike over his shoulders, his thin cigarette held elegantly, Russian-style, between his thumb and forefinger.)*—formerly of Odessa's Marinsky Theatre and the Second Avenue Yiddish Classic Art Players; now, in leaner times, appearing solo and at club meetings as *all* of the Second Avenue Yiddish Classic Art Players, some ascribing this to the Depression and others to the inconvenience of having to work on a stage cluttered by other actors.

(As Zaretsky arrives at the bar, Eddie, without turning to him, and clearly enacting the ritual of many mornings, briskly pours half a tumbler of straight vodka, places it behind himself on the bar, still without turn-

*ing, and quickly resumes his busy preparations. Za-
retsky, with a sweep of his arm and a sharp flick of his
wrist, downs the vodka in one efficient swallow; he
places the empty tumbler with a snap on the bar,
pauses a moment—then lets go with a truly hair-
raising, shattering, siren-like scream of pain. The
scream, obviously part of the ritual, is in no way ac-
knowledged by Charlie, the Kid in the Stroller, Eddie
—who continues with his back to Zaretsky—or
Zaretsky himself. Silence again for a moment or two.)*

Zaretsky *(elegant Russian accent, to Kid in Stroller
and Eddie)*: Chaim, Itzik, God had two great ideas:
beautiful women, and how to drink a potato.

*(He crosses briskly to his usual table at center, opens
his newspaper—one of several Yiddish journals he carries with him along with an old carpetbag-style valise
—and sits deep into his chair and a world of his own,
encircled by his morning vodka and "The Jewish Daily
Forward"; all this as Charlie moves towards the stairway, looks up at Apartment, continues talking.)*

Charlie: Very important distinction between living behind your store and living *above* it—two years ago
we'd made the big move from "living in back" on Rivington to "living over" on Canal; surely goodness and
mercy and the Big Bucks would soon be following us.

Zaretsky *(not looking up from paper)*: For those interested, from today's "Jewish Daily Forward," an item:
"Yesterday morning in Geneva, Stefan Lux, a forty-

eight-year-old Jewish journalist from Prague, stood up in the midst of a League of Nations meeting, pulled an automatic pistol from his briefcase, shouted 'Avenol, Avenol,' and shot himself in the chest. In his briefcase a letter to Secretary General Joseph Avenol stating that he has killed himself publicly to awaken the League's conscience to the plight of the Jews in the Reich." *(Silence; waits for response, then turns page.)* I thank you all for your attention.

Eddie *(slaps the bar with his towel)*: O.K., Charlie, I know what's *up*, I know what you're *doin'* . . . *(Turns to Stroller, smiling.)* And I *like* it! *(Approaching Stroller with diaper and towel.)* You're *my kid* and you're not gonna say what you gotta say till you're damn good and *ready.* So I say *this* to you—don't let nobody push you around, and I include *myself* in that remark; got it? Because I would be tickled pink if the first goddamn sentence you ever said was: "Charlie Goldberg don't take shit from *no*body!" *(Taking dirty diaper out of Stroller.)* O.K., now I see you got a hold of your dick there. This don't bother me, be my guest. There's many schools of thought on grabbing your dick, pro and con. Me, I'm pro. I say, go to it, it's *your dick.* What you hope for is that someday some kind person out there will be as interested in it as you are. What you got a hold of there is optimism itself, what you got there in your hand is blind hope, which is the best kind. *(Grips edge of Stroller.)* Everybody says to me, "Hey, four bars into the toilet, *enough, forget* it, Eddie—a steady job tendin' *bar*, Eddie, maybe managin' a class place"—I say, "I don't work for *no*body, baby, this ain't no employee's personality; I sweat, but I sweat for my *own*." *(Deposits slug in Jukebox, making selection.)* And I ain't talking about no gin-mill, kid, I ain't talkin' about saloons and stand-up bars—I'm talkin' about what we got *here*, Charlie . . . I'm talkin' about America . . . *(From the Jukebox we begin to hear a full Chorus and Orchestra doing a gorgeous rendition of "America, the Beautiful," all strings and harps and lovely echoing voices.)* We give 'em *America*, Charlie— *(Takes in the place with a sweep of his hand as the Music fills the room.)* We give 'em a Moose, we give 'em George Washington, we give 'em the red-white-and-blue, and mostly we give 'em, bar none, the greatest American invention of the last ten years—*Cocktails*! *(He flips a switch, illuminating the entire bar area, the mirror glows, a long strip of bulbs running the length of the shelf at the base of the mirror lights up the row of several dozen exotically colored cocktail-mix bottles; he points at the Stroller.)* O.K., *Canal* Street, y'say— that's not a cocktail *clientele* out there, these are people who would suck after-shave lotion out of a wet washcloth—*(Advancing on Stroller as Music builds.)* *Nossir!* The trick here, all ya gotta remember, is nobody's equal but everybody *wants* to be—downtown slobs lookin' for uptown class, goddamn Greenhorns lookin' to turn Yankee—New York style American Cocktails, Charlie! We liquor up these low-life nickel-dimers just long enough to bankroll an Uptown lounge—

Chorus and Orchestra *(a Soprano solo rising delicately as Eddie kneels next to Stroller)*:

". . . Thine alabaster cities gleam,
Undimmed by human tears . . ."

Eddie: *Yessir*, that's where we're *goin'*, you and me;
I'm lookin' *Up*town, kid, Madison, Lex—I got a *plan*,
see, I'm *thinkin'*—*(Rising with the lush Soprano.)* because there's only two ways a Jew *gets* Uptown; wanna
get outa here, kid, you gotta *punch* your way out or
think your way out. You're Jewish you gotta be
smarter than everybody else; or cuter or faster or funnier. Or tougher. Because, basically, they want to kill
you; this is true maybe thirty, thirty-five hundred
years now and is not likely to change next Tuesday.
It's not they don't want you in Moscow, or Kiev, or
Lodz, or Jersey City: it's the earth, they don't want you
on the *earth* is the problem; so the trick is to become
necessary. If they need you they don't kill you. Naturally, they're gonna hate you for needing you, but that
beats they don't need you and they kill you. Got it?
(His arms spread wide in conclusion.) This, kid . . . is
the whole story.

Chorus and Orchestra *(Full Chorus and Strings as
the Music comes to a lush finale)*:
". . . From sea to shining sea!"

Zaretsky *(not looking up from newspaper)*: Itzik, the
only Jew in this room being persecuted is two years
old.

Eddie: You, Actor; quiet.

Zaretsky: Fortunately, he understands very few of your dangerously misguided words, Itzik.

Eddie: *Eddie*, goddamnit, *Eddie*!

Zaretsky: Please, enough; I am not feeling very vigorous this morning. You have kept an entire household awake all night with your terrible noises.

Eddie: Terrible *noises*? I'm up all night doin' a complete refurbish on the place, single-handed, top to bottom; I don't hear no comment. *(Continuing work behind bar.)* Guy *lives* here should show an interest.

Zaretsky *(he puts down his paper; looks about, nodding thoughtfully)*: Ah, yes. Ah, yes . . . Tell me, Eddie; what period are you attempting to capture here?

Eddie: Early American.

Zaretsky: I see. How early?

Eddie: Revolutionary *War*, shmuck. From now on this place, it's always gonna be the Fourth of July here. How about that Moose?

Zaretsky *(leans back, studying it)*: Ah, yes; the Moose.

Eddie: How's it look to ya?

Zaretsky: Shocked. Completely shocked to be here. One minute he's trotting freely through the sweet green forest—next thing he knows he's staring out at a third-rate saloon on Canal Street; forever. Yes, shocked and dismayed to be here, in Early America. As am I, *Eddie. (He lifts up his newspaper.)*

Eddie *(turns sharply from bar)*: *Greenhorn!* Greenhorn bullshit! You came here a Grinneh, you *stayed* a Grinneh. *Grinneh*—you were *then*, you are *now*, and you always *will* be! *(Leans towards him.)* I *hear* ya, what kinda *noise* is that? "I don't feel wery wigorous"—what *is* that? Ya don't have to *do* that, ya *know* ya don't, you could get *rid* of that. I come here after *you* did, listen to me. Check the patter. I read Winchell, I go to the movies, I know the score—

(During these last few moments, Gusta has entered from the Apartment above and stopped about halfway down the stairs, her attention caught by the Moose head; small, perpetually busy, near forty, she carries two large pots of just-cooked food, each about a third of her size.)

Gusta: Eddie, there's an animal on the wall.

Eddie: It's a Moose.

Gusta: All right, I'll believe you; it's a Moose. Why is it on the wall?

Eddie: For one thing, it's a Moose *head*—

Gusta: Believe me, I didn't think the rest of it was sticking out into Canal Street.

Charlie: Hey . . . she's actually *funny* . . . *(To Eddie:) Laugh*, will ya?

Gusta *(crossing quickly to Kitchen)*: My favorite, personally, was "Cap'n Ed's Place"; I liked those waves you painted on the mirror, and your sailor hat, *that* was a beauty.

Eddie: *Captain's* hat, it was a *Captain's* hat—*(Quietly, to Stroller:)* Why do I talk to her? Why? *Tell* me. Do *you* know?

Gusta *(chuckling, setting pots down on stove)*: Meanwhile, I see so far nobody showed up for the Revolution.

Eddie: Because we ain't *open* yet! *Eight* o'clock, that's the law, I stick to the rules. *(Points to framed Roosevelt photo.)* Like F.D.R. says, in that way he's got—"It is by strict adherence to the rules that we shall avoid descent to the former evils of the saloon."

Gusta *(indicates F.D.R. photo)*: Look at that smile, the man him*self* is half-drunk mosta the time. Your Roosevelt, he says, "There is nothing to fear but fear itself." What, that's not *enough*?

Eddie: Not another *word*—not another word against the man in my place!

Gusta (*approaching Stroller with bit of food on stirring spoon, singing softly, an old Yiddish lullaby*):
"Oif'n pripitchok, brent a faieril,
Un in shtub iz heys,
Un der rebe lerent kleyne kinderlach
Dem alef beys . . ."

Charlie (*at Kitchen, inhaling the memory*): That food . . . Brisket Tzimmes, Lokshen Kugel . . .

Gusta (*sitting next to Stroller, gently*):
"Zetje kinderlach, gedenktje taiere,
Voseer lerent daw . . ."
    (*Zaretsky starts to hum along with her.*)
"Zogtje noch amol, un take noch amol,
Kometz alef aw . . ."

Eddie: Hey, you people want lullabies, what the hell's wrong with "Rock-a-bye Baby"? A good, solid, American hit—

Gusta (*softly, reaching spoon into Stroller*):
"Zogtje noch amol, un take noch amol,
Kometz alef aw . . ."

Charlie (*softly, kneeling near her*): She's young . . . she's so young . . .

Gusta (*smiling sweetly*): Now sing along with me, darling; just "Alef aw" . . . (*Singing, Charlie behind her urging the Kid to respond.*) "Kometz alef aw . . . alef aw . . ." (*No response; she shrugs.*) A shtik fleysh mit oygen. (*Goes back to Kitchen.*)

Charlie: My mother has just referred to me as "a piece of meat with two eyes."

Eddie: That's why the kid don't talk, he don't know what *language* to speak!

Gusta (*laughing to herself, stacking dishes on bar*): Eddie, Ethel called me with two good ones this morning—I mean, *good* ones—

Eddie: Not now, Gloria. Gimme the Specials. (*Turns to blackboard over bar marked "Today's Specials," picks up chalk.*)

Gusta: So this old Jewish mama, lonely, a widow— her fancy son can't be bothered, sends her a parrot to keep her company—

Eddie: The *Specials*, Gloria—

Gusta: This is a five-hundred-dollar parrot, speaks six languages, including Russian and Yiddish—

Eddie: The pots, the pots, what's in the *pots*?!

Gusta: A week goes by, he don't hear from her, calls up, "Mama, did you get the parrot?" "Yes," she says, "thank you, Sonny; *delicious*." (*Breaks up, laughing* *happily, turns heat down under pots.)* Eddie, you want the Specials?

Eddie *(to Stroller)*: Come on, Charlie, *tell* me, why do I . . . ? Yeah.

Gusta: O.K., in the big pot, Brisket Tzimmes with honey, carrot, sweet potato, a dash raisins.

Eddie *(writing in bold letters on blackboard)*: "Mulligan Stew."

Gusta *(removing apron)*: Next to it, still simmering, we got Lokshen Kugel with apple, cinnamon, raisin, a sprinkle nuts.

Eddie *(thinks a minute, then writes)*: "Hot Apple Pie."

Charlie *(whispering)*: No, Pop . . . no . . .

Gusta *(taking school notebook from shelf near phone)*: Now I go to Mr. Katz. Don't forget, in a half-hour, you'll turn me off the Lokshen please.

Eddie: Twelve *years*—twelve years of English with Mr. Katz you're still sayin' "turn me off the Lokshen"!

Gusta *(going to entrance door)*: It's not just English at the Alliance, we *discuss* things; politics, *Jewish* things.

Eddie: Goddamn *Commie*, that Katz; he's open Washington's Birthday, *Lincoln's, now* he's teaching on July Fourth!

Gusta: He's not a Communist; he's only an Anarchist.

Eddie: What's the difference?

Gusta: Louder, and fewer holidays. *(Breaks up again, laughing, opens door, waves to Stroller.)* Bye-bye, Charlie, when Mama comes back we chapn a bisl luft in droysen, yes?

Charlie *(to Audience)*: "Catch a bit of air outside."

Eddie: *English*, for Chrissakes, *English*—

Gusta *(as she exits, laughing)*: "Delicious," she says, "delicious" . . .

Eddie *(shouting at door)*: English—*(Turning sharply to Zaretsky.)* English! The *two* of ya, the *mouth* on ya, kid's all screwed up, thinks he's livin' in Odessa; meanwhile ya give my *joint* a bad feel. Goddamn Jewish *news*papers all over the place—what're we, advertisin' for *rabbis* here? *(Points to Jukebox.)* Goodness of my heart I put some Jew Music on the Box for ya—all I ask ya don't play it business hours or in fronta my kids. Next thing I know Jack says you're playin' "Rumania" straight through his *shift* last night. The two of ya, I swear, you're discouragin' the proper clientele here, and that's the fact of the matter. Jews don't drink; this is a law of nature, a law of nature and of commerce. (*He slaps the bar with finality; then resumes his work. Silence for a moment.*)

Zaretsky (*singing, from behind his newspaper, a thick brogue*):
 "Oh, Dan-ny Boy,
 The pipes, the pipes are callin' . . ."

Eddie (*leans forward on bar*): Damn *right*, Mister—damn *right* that's who drinks! You can't sell shoes to people who ain't got no *feet*, pal!

Zaretsky (*singing*):
 "From glen to glen . . ."

Eddie: Hey, far *be* it! Far be it from me to discuss makin' a living! (*Coming out from behind bar.*) What's that foreign mouth been *gettin'* you, Zaretsky? A once-a-month shot in the Mountains puttin' retired Yidd-lach to sleep with old Sholem Aleichem stories? *Pushkin* for the Literatniks? What? When's the last time you saw somebody in a Yiddish theater under a hundred who wasn't dragged there by his Zayde? Read the handwritin' on the goddamn *marquee*, amigo; it's *over*. Gotta give 'em what they *want*, see. That's the Promised Land, pal—find out what they want and *promise* it to them. (*Takes frozen vodka from under bar.*) Yessir—(*Pouring half-glass; to Stroller:*) A toast to that, Charlie!

Charlie: Pop never drank—except to propose a toast, and that toast was always to the same thing . . .

Eddie (*holding glass aloft, towards front door*): The new place, Charlie . . . to today, the Openin' Day . . . I lift my lamp beside the Golden Door; bring me your tired, your poor, your drinkers, your winos, your alkies, your—

Zaretsky (*lowers his newspaper*): I knew a man once, Itzik Goldberg, with the colors of Odessa and the spirit of a Jew, and I saw this man turn white before my eyes, white as milk—Grade A, pasteurized, homogenized, American *milk*!

Eddie (*softly, to Stroller*): Very sad, Charlie; a dyin' man with a dead language and no place to go. (*Downs vodka, turns sharply, shouting.*) Check me out, Actor —current cash problems I gotta *tolerate* your crap— soon as this place hits you're out on the *street*, inside a year you're sleepin' in *sinks*, baby; this is a *warning*! (*Slaps glass down.*)

Zaretsky (*shouting, fiercely*): And a warning to *you*, sir; I shall no longer countenance these threats!

Charlie: This exchange, a holler more or less, took place every day, except Sunday, at approximately Seven-Fifteen A.M. After which, they would usually— (*Sees his father pouring another vodka; Charlie is suddenly anxious.*) Oh, shit, another one . . .

Eddie (*downs second vodka; then, quietly, to Stroller*): Hey, y'know, anything you got to say to me, nobody's gonna know, it's all strictly confidential. (*Takes small red ball from Stroller, tosses it back in; pleasantly:*) There ya go, pick up the ball and give it back to Papa. (*Silence.*) Pick it up . . . (*A sudden, frightened whisper escapes him.*) Oh, kid, don't be dumb . . . you're not gonna turn out to be dumb, are ya? (*Pause.*) Those eyes; don't look at me like that, Charlie . . . (*Sits on chair next to Stroller, gazing into it.*) You got your grandpa's sweet face, see . . . exactly, to the letter; the soft eyes and the gentle, gentle smile, and it scares the shit outa me. His head in the Talmud and his foot in the grave, the guy come here and got creamed, kid. Not you, Charlie; I'm gonna do good here, but you're gonna do better. There's two kinda guys come off the boat: the Go-Getters and the Ground-Kissers. Your grandpa, though a better soul never walked the earth, was to all intents and purposes, a putz; a darling man and a born Ground-Kisser. In *Hamburg*, in the harbor, we ain't even *sailed* yet and the kissing begins: he kisses the gangplank, he kisses the doorway, he kisses the scummy goddamn *steer*age *floor* of the S.S. Pennland. Nine hundred miles we walk to get to the boat, just him and me, I gotta handle all the bribes. Ten years *old*, I gotta grease my way across the Russian Empire, he don't know how. *Fine* points, this is all he ever knew: *fine* points. *My* grandpa, one o' them solid-steel rabbis, gives Pop a sweet send-off back in Odessa: "Have a good trip, Solomon," he says; "eat kosher or die." So twenty-six days on the boat Pop eats little pieces of bread they give ya with kosher stamps on 'em and a coupla prayed-on potatoes; *I'm* scroungin' everything in sight to stay alive. *Fine* points! Pop loses thirty pounds, *he's* a wreck but the *lips*, the lips are in great shape, the lips are working! New York harbor, he's kissin' the deck, he's blowin' kisses to Lady Liberty, he's kissin' the *barge* that takes us to Ellis Island. On the mainland, forget it, the situation is turnin' pornographic. Twenty-eight blocks to his brother on Rivington—some people took a trolley, *we* went by lip. On Grand Street I come over to him, this little rail of a man, I say, "Get off your knees, Pop; stand up, everybody's *lookin'*, what the hell're ya doin'?" Looks at me, his eyes are sweet and wet, he says, "It's God's will that we come here, Itzik. I show my love for his intentions . . ." *Fine* points! *(Suddenly rises, bangs his fist on the table next to him, showing the effects of his vodka.)* Goddamn *fine* points . . . *(Gradually turning towards Zaretsky, who remains behind his newspaper.)* Opens a joint here on Rivington: Solomon's Tavern. The man is closed Friday night and Saturday by God's law and Sunday by New York's—the income is brought by Elijah every Passover. Comes Prohibition, he sticks to the letter; coffee, soda, three-two beer and no booze—every joint in the neighborhood's got teapots fulla gin and bourbon in coffee cups, we're scratchin' for nickels and lovin' God's intentions. A summer night, late, they come to sell him bootleg: two little Ginzos and this big Mick hench with eyes that died. "Oh, *no*," says Papa the Putz, "not *me*. Against the *law*," he says—he's *ed*ucatin' these yo-yo meat grinders, right?—he says he's callin' the cops and the Feds and he's goin' to all the local congregations to talk his fellow Jews outa buyin' or sellin' bootleg. "Do it and you're a dead Yid," says the hench. Pop don't get the message—no, he's got his *own* message now—in a week he hits every landsman's bar he can find, he's tellin' 'em they gotta respect where God has sent them; gets to five, six shuls that week, *three* on Saturday, he's givin' goddamn public *speeches* in Rutgers Square! A five-foot-six, hundred-and-twenty-pound Jew has selected Nineteen Twenty-One in America as the perfect time to be anti-gangster! What the *hell* did he think was gonna protect him? The *cops*? His *God*? By Sunday morning he is, of course, dead in Cortlandt Alley over here with his skull smashed in. They hustle me over there at Seven A.M. to say if it's him; I know before I get there. When they turn him over I don't look—it's not the bashed-in head I'm afraid of; I'm afraid I'll see from his lips that with the last breath he was kissing the dust in Cortlandt Alley. *(Moving briskly up to bar.)* The *perfection* of it—his Jewish God had his soul and America had his heart, he died a devout and patriotic *putz*! *(Reflexively splashes vodka into glass, downs it in a gulp, slaps glass onto bar. A moment; he chuckles.)* So he don't get thrown outa heaven, he gives two bucks to this place, the Sons of Moses, to guarantee his soul gets prayed for; for two dollars they send me a card every year for the rest of my *life* to remind me to light Pop's Yahrzeit candle and do the Kaddish for him; I can't get halfway through the prayer without sayin' "Go to hell, Pop." I look at the card, I see the alley. And wherever I live, the card comes. Wherever you go, they find you, those Sons of Moses. The putz won't leave me be. He wouldn't shut up *then* and he won't shut up now . . . he won't shut up . . . he won't shut up . . . he won't shut *up*—

(In one sudden, very swift movement, he kicks over the bar-table next to him, its contents clattering to the floor; Charlie, taken completely by surprise, leaps to his feet in his booth as the round table rolls part-way across the bar-room floor. Eddie, quite still, watches the table roll to a stop. Silence for a moment. Zaretsky lowers his newspaper.)

Zaretsky *(raising his glass, proudly)*: To Solomon Goldberg . . . who I saw speak in Rutgers Square against drinking and crime to an audience of drunks and criminals. Completely foolish and absolutely thrilling. We need a million Jews like him. *(Downs shot, turns sharply.)* You came to the Melting Pot, sir, and *melted* . . . melted *away. (Slaps glass down.)*

Eddie *(turns to Zaretsky; quietly)*: Whatsa matter, you *forget*, pal? *(Moving slowly towards Zaretsky's table.)* Wasn't that *you* I seen runnin' bare-ass down Dalnitz-kaya Street—a dozen Rooski Goys and a coupla Greek Orthodox with goddamn *sabers* right behind, lookin' to slice somethin' Jewish off ya? Only thirty years ago, you were no kid *then*, moving pretty good considerin'. Did they catch ya, pal? What'd they slice off ya, Za-retsky? Your memory? They held my grandpa down under his favorite acacia tree and pulled his beard out—his beard, a rabbi's honor—they're tearin' it outa his face a chunk at a time, him screamin' in this gar-den behind his shul, they grabbed us *all* there that

Saturday comin' outa morning prayers. This chubby
one is whirlin' a saber over his head, faster and faster
till it whistles—I know this guy, I seen him waitin'
tables at the Café Fankoni—"I'm takin' your skull-cap
off," he says to my brother Heshy; one whistlin' swing,
he slices it off along with the top of Heshy's skull,
scalpin' him. Heshy's very proud of this yarmulkeh,
he's Bar Mitzvah a month before and wears it the entire Shabes—he's got his hands on his head, the blood
is runnin' through his fingers, he's already dead, he
still runs around the garden like a chicken for maybe
thirty seconds before he drops, hollerin' "Voo iz mine
yarmulkeh? . . . Voo iz mine yarmulkeh?" The kid is
more afraid of not being Jewish than not being alive.
(At Zaretsky's table, leaning towards him.) My mother,
they cut her ears off; her ears, go figure it, what was
Jewish about *them*? Regardless, she bled to death in
the garden before it got dark, ranting like a child by
then, really nuts. The guy's caftan flies open, the one
doin' the job on Ma, I see an Odessa police uniform
underneath, this is just a regular beat cop from Pri-
morsky Boulevard, and the waiter too, just another
person; but they were all screaming, these guys—
louder than my family even—and their women too,
watching, screaming, "Molodyets!" "Natchinai!" "good
man," "go to it," like ladies I seen at ringside, only
happier, all screaming with their men in that garden,
all happy to find the bad guys. *(Sits opposite Zaretsky.)*
This Cossack's holdin' me down, he's makin' me watch
while they do the ear-job on Ma. "Watch, Zhid, watch!
Worse to watch than to die!" He holds me, he's got my
arms, it feels like I'm drowning. Since then, nobody

holds me down, Zaretsky, nobody. I don't even like hugs. *(Grips Zaretsky's wrist, urgently.)* The October Pogrom, how could you forget? Livin' with us two *years* now, you don't even *mention* it. You wanna run around bein' Mister Jewish—that's *your* lookout—but you leave me and my kids *out* of it. *(Rises, moving briskly to bar.)* I got my own deal with God, see; Joey does a few hours a week o' Hebrew School, just enough to make the Bar Mitzvah shot—same with Charlie—I hit the shul Rosh Hashana, maybe Yom Kippur, and sometimes Fridays Gloria does the candle routine; and that's *it*. You treat God like you treat *any* dangerous looney—keep him calm and stay on his *good* side. Meanwhile . . . *(Takes folded legal document from cash register, smiling proudly.)* Today, today the Jew lid comes off my boys. *(Striding back to Zaretsky's table, opening document with a flourish.)* Check it out, Anton, you're the first to know—*(Reads from document:)* "Southern District Court, State of New York, the Honorable Alfred Gladstone, presiding. Application approved, this Third day of July, of the year Nineteen Hundred and Thirty-Six; Change of Family Name—" *(Holding document aloft.)* Yessir; so long, Goldberg; as of One P.M. yesterday you been livin' here with the *Ross* family—outside, take note, the sign says "Eddie Ross' Golden Door"; shit, I just say it out *loud*, I get a shiver. *(Sits next to Zaretsky, pointing to photos over bar.)* "Ross," yessir—honor o' Barney "One-Punch" Ross *and* Mr. Franklin Delano Roosevelt, friend of the Jews, God bless 'im. *(Leans towards Zaretsky.)* Goldberg sat down with ya, pal . . . *(Slaps table, stands up.)*

but Ross rises. *(Striding briskly up towards bar.)* And he's got business to do!

Zaretsky *(after a moment, quietly)*: You didn't mention the feathers . . . *(Eddie stops, turns to him; Zaretsky remains at his table, looking away.)* All the goose-feathers, Itzik. Three days exactly, the perfect pogrom; and on the fourth day, in the morning, a terrible silence and feathers everywhere, a carpet of goose-feathers on every street. The Jews of the Moldavanka, even the poorest of them, had goose-feather mattresses and pillows; and this made the Christians somehow very angry. So from every home they dragged out mattresses, pillows, ripped them open and threw the feathers in the streets; thousands of mattresses, millions of feathers, feathers everywhere and so white and the blood so red on them, and the sky so very blue as only could be in Odessa by the sea. All beautiful and horrible like a deadly snow had fallen in the night. This is what I remember. In the big synagogue on Catherine Street they had broken even the highest windows, and these windows stared like blinded eyes over the Moldavanka. And below there are feathers in all the acacia trees on Catherine Street, white feathers in the branches, as though they had bloomed again in October, as though the trees too had gone mad. And crazier still that morning, waddling down the street towards me, an enormous fat man, like from the circus, laughing. I watch him, silent like a balloon on the soft feathers, into one empty Jewish house and then another he goes, growing fatter as he comes, and now closer I see the face of the Greek, Poldaris, from the tobacco shop, and he is wearing one atop the other the suits and cloaks of dead Jews. No, Mr. Ross, they didn't catch me, and no, I didn't forget; this morning even, the fat Poldaris follows me still, laughing, waiting for my clothes. *(Turns to Eddie.)* A picture remains—a picture more disturbing even than the one of Eddie Cantor in black-face you have hung in my room. That first night I am hiding in the loft above the horses in the Fire Station and I see on the street below me young Grillspoon kneeling in the feathers before his house, his hands clasped heavenward, like so. He pleads for his life to be spared by five members of the Holy Brotherhood who stand about him—this group has sworn vengeance on those who tortured their Savior upon the cross, Grillspoon obviously amongst them, and each carries a shovel for this purpose. Now, a Jew does not kneel when he prays, nor does he clasp his hands, and it becomes clear that poor Grillspoon is imitating the manner of Christian prayer, hoping to remind them of themselves. The actor in me sees that this man is fiercely auditioning for the role of Christian for them—and these men for the moment stand aside from him, leaning on their shovels as they watch his performance. Presently, however, they proceed to rather efficiently beat him to death with their shovels. Talk about bad reviews, eh? *(Rises, takes a step towards Eddie.)* Unfortunately, you have decided that the only way to become somebody in this country is first to become no one at all. You are kneeling in your goose-feathers, Mr. Ross. *You*, you who profess to be such a violent Anti-Kneeler.

Eddie: Go to hell, Actor. *(Turns away sharply, starts briskly stacking glasses behind the bar.)*

Zaretsky *(moving steadily towards Eddie)*: For God's *sake*, Itzik, they had to *take* your grandfather's beard and your brother's yarmulkeh—but what is yours you will *give* away; and like poor Grillspoon you will reap the disaster of a second-rate Christian imitation. And as a pro*fessional*, I *swear* to you, Itzik—*(bangs his fist on the bar)* you are *definitely wrong for the part*!

(Eddie wheels about sharply, about to speak—but Joey Goldberg bursts in from the Apartment above, speaking as he enters, cutting Eddie off; a tough-looking ten-year old, he bounds down the stairs, his Hebrew School books tied with a belt and slung over his shoulder, heading directly for his morning task—a tray of "set-ups" on the bar.)

Joey: Hey, sorry I'm late, Pop—

Zaretsky: Jussel! A guten tog, Jussel!

Joey: A guten tog, Professor! Vos harst du fun der Rialto!

Eddie *(anguished, slapping bar)*: My God, they got *him* doin' it now too . . .

Charlie *(fondly)*: Hey, Joey . . .

Joey *(passing Stroller)*: How ya doin', kid?

Charlie *(to Audience)*: Besides me, Joey loved only two things in this world: the New York Giants and the Yiddish Theatre; for my brother had witnessed two miracles in his life—Carl Hubbell's screwball, and Mr. Zaretsky's King Lear.

Joey *(carrying set-ups to center table, spotting valise)*: Hey, Mr. Zaretsky . . . we got the *satchel* . . .

Zaretsky: Yes, Jussel—*(grandly lifting valise)* today a journey to Detroit, in Michigan, there presenting my solo concert—"Pieces of Gold from the Golden Years."

Eddie: Hey, Joey, I got the *Moose* up, see—

Joey *(a quick glance at it)*: Yeah, great—*(To Zaretsky, fascinated:)* "Pieces Of Gold" . . . what's the lineup on that one?

Zaretsky *(opening valise)*: The Program, as follows—

Eddie: Joey, the *set*-ups—

Zaretsky: *(his arms outstretched, setting the scene)*: A simple light—possibly blue—reveals a humble satchel, and within—*(Joey and Charlie, their arms outstretched, saying the words with him)*—a world of Yiddish Theatre!

Eddie: The *set*-ups, Joey—

(Joey continuing absently, sporadically, to place set-ups on tables, his gaze fixed on Zaretsky's performance.)

Zaretsky *(takes tarnished gold crown from valise, placing it on his head)*: To begin—

Joey: The old guy with the daughters!

Zaretsky: Der Kenig Lear, of course! *(Drops crown into valise.)* Three minutes: an appetizer. And then— *(removes a battered plaster skull; studies it, fondly)* "Zuch in vey, umglicklickeh Yorick . . . ich hub im gut gekennt, Horatio . . ." *(Briskly exchanging skull for an ornate dagger; a thoughtful gaze, whispering:)* "Tzu zein, oder nicht tzu zein . . . dus is die fragge . . ." *(Replacing dagger with a small, knotted rope.)* The bonds of Sidney Carton, the shadow of the guillotine . . . *(Looks up; softly:)* "Es is a fiel, fiel besera zach vus ich tu yetst, vus ich hub amol getune . . ." *(Swiftly replacing rope with the fur hat of a Cossack general.)* The "Kiddush HaShem" of Sholem Asch, sweeping drama of seventeenth-century Cossack pogroms; condensed. *(Drops Cossack hat into valise.)* When they have recovered—*(Places yarmulkeh delicately on his head; directs this at Eddie, busy behind bar.)* Sholem Aleichem's "Hard to Be a Jew" . . . humor and sudden shadows. *(Removes yarmulkeh; his arms outstretched, grandly.)* In conclusion, of course, my twelve-minute version of "The Dybbuk," all in crimson light if equipment available; I play all parts . . . including title role. *(A moment; then he bows his head as though before a huge Jewish audience in a grand hall; he speaks qui-*

etly:) I hear the applause . . . *(He looks out.)* I see their faces, so familiar . . . and once again I have eluded the fat Poldaris. He shall not have my clothes. *(Silence for a moment; then he picks up his valise, striding briskly to the front door.)* Give up my Yiddish Theatre? No, Itzik, I don't think so. Yes, overblown, out of date, soon to disappear. But then, so am I. *(Turns at door.)* I go now to the tailor, Zellick, who repairs my robes for Lear. Good morning to you, Jussel; and good morning to you, Mr. Ross, and, of course, my regards to your wife, Betsy.

(Zaretsky exits; Eddie instantly intensifies his work behind the bar; Joey not moving, looking off at front door, still in awe.)

Eddie: *Fake*-o, Joey, I'm tellin' ya—fake-o four-flushin' phony. Man don't make no sense, any manner, shape or form.

Joey: You should see the way he does that *Dybbuk* guy, Pop, he really—

Eddie: Joey, the set-ups—what happened to the goddamn *set*-ups here! And the *mail*, kid, ya *forgot* it yesterday.

Joey *(picks up books)*: Gonna be late for Hebrew, Pop, it's almost Eight—

Eddie: Then ya shouldn'ta hung around watchin' Cary Grant so long.

Joey: Ten to Eight, Pop, gotta get goin'—

Eddie: Bring in the *mail* first, you got obligations here, Mister.

Joey *(puts books down)*: O.K., O.K. . . . *(Passing Stroller.)* He say anything today?

Eddie: All quiet on the western front.

Joey *(looking into Stroller)*: Don't worry about him, Pop; look at the eyes, he's gettin' *everything*. *(As he exits.)* He's smart, this kid; very smart, like me.

Eddie: And modest *too*, I bet. *(Alone now; he pauses for a moment, then goes to the Stroller, peers in thoughtfully.)* Everything?

Charlie: Every word, Pop.

Eddie *(leans forward)*: Hey, what the hell're ya *doin'*? This ain't no time to go to *sleep*. You just got *up*, for God's sake—*(Shaking the Stroller.)* Let's show a little *courtesy* here, a little common goddamn *courtesy*. *(Stops.)* Out. He's *out*. I either got Calvin Coolidge with his dick in his fist or he's *out*!

Joey *(entering, thoughtfully, with stack of mail)*: Pop, the sign outside, it says "Ross" on it . . .

Eddie: That's our new name, you're gonna love it; honor o' Barney himself. *(Takes mail, starts going through it.)*

Joey: You mean not just for the place, but actually our new name?

Eddie: All done; legit and legal, kid, Al Gladstone presidin'—*(Takes envelope from mail.)* Son of a bitch, the Sons of Moses, Pop's Yahrzeit again . . .

Joey: So my name is Joe Ross? That's my name now? Joe Ross? Very . . . brief, that name.

Eddie *(studying blue card from envelope)*: Fifteen *years*, they find me every time, it's the Royal Mounted Rabbis . . .

Joey: Joe Ross; it starts—it's *over*.

Eddie: Hey, *Hebrew* school—

Joey *(suddenly alarmed)*: Jeez, went right outa my mind—*(Grabs Hebrew texts, races for door, slapping yarmulkeh on his head.)*

Eddie: *Wait* a minute—*(Points to yarmulkeh.)* Where ya goin' with *that* on your head? What're ya, crazy? Ya gonna go eight blocks through Little Italy and Irish-town, passin' right through goddamn *Polack* Street, with *that* on your head? How many times I gotta tell ya, kid—that is *not* an outdoor garment. That is an indoor garment *only*. Why don't ya wear a sign on your head says, "Please come kick the shit outa me"? You put it on in Hebrew School, where it belongs.

Joey: Pop, I don't—

Eddie: I'm tellin' ya *once* more—stow the yammy, kid. *Stow* it.

Joey *(whips yarmulkeh off, shoves it in pocket)*: O.K., O.K. *(Starts towards door.)* I just don't see why I gotta be ashamed.

Eddie: I'm not askin' ya to be ashamed. I'm askin' ya to be smart. *(Sees something in mail as Joey opens door; sharply:)* Hold it—

Joey: Gotta go, Pop—

Eddie: *Hold* it right there—

Joey: Pop, this Tannenbaum, he's a killer—

Eddie *(looking down at mail; solemnly)*: I got information here says you ain't *seein'* Tannenbaum this morning. I got information here says you ain't even headed for Hebrew School right now. *(Silence for a moment. Joey remains in doorway.)* C'mere, we gotta talk.

Joey *(approaching cautiously, keeping at a safe distance)*: Hey . . . no whackin', Pop . . .

Eddie: I got this note here; says—*(Takes small piece of cardboard from mail, reads:)* "Dear Sheenie Bastard. Back of Carmine's, Remind you, Jewshit Joe, Eight O'Clock A.M., Be there. Going to make Hamburger out of Goldberger—S.D." Bastard is spelled here B-A-S-T-I-D; this and the humorous remarks I figure the fine mind of the wop, DeSapio. *(After a moment, looks up, slaps bar.)* And I wanna tell ya *good* luck, *glad* you're goin', you're gonna *nail* 'im, you're gonna *finish* 'im, you're gonna murder 'im—

Joey: Wait a minute—it's O.K.? Really?

Eddie: —and here'a couple pointers how to do so.

Joey: Pointers? *Pointers?* . . . I need a *shot*gun, Pop; DeSapio's near twice my size, fourteen years *old*—

Eddie: Hey, far *be* it! Far be it from me to give pointers—a guy got twenty-six bouts under his belt, *twelve* professional—

Joey: Yeah, but this DeSapio, he really *hates* me, this kid; he hated me the minute he *saw* me. He says we killed Christ, us Jews.

Eddie: They was *all* Jews there, kid, everybody; Christ, His mother, His whole crowd—you tell him there was a buncha Romans there too, makes him *directly related* to the guys done the actual hit!

Joey: I *told* him that, Pop—that's when he *whacked* me.

Eddie: And I bet you whacked him back, which is appropriate; *no* shit from *no*body, ya stuck to your *guns*, kid—

Joey: So why're we hidin' then? How come we're "Ross" all of a sudden? *(With an edge:)* Or maybe Ross is just our *out*door name, and Goldberg's still our indoor name.

Eddie: *Hey*—

Joey: I don't *get* it, this mean we're not Jewish anymore?

Eddie: Of *course* we're still Jewish; we're just not gonna push it.

Joey *(checking watch)*: Jeez—three minutes to Eight, Pop, takes five to get there, he's gonna think I'm chicken—*(Starts towards door.)*

Eddie: *One* minute for two pointers; let 'im wait, he'll get anxious—

Joey: He's *not anxious*, Pop, I promise ya—

Eddie: Now, these pointers is based on my observations o' your natural talents: the bounce, the eye, the smarts—

Joey (*protesting*): Pop—

Eddie: C'mon, I seen ya take out Itchy Halloran with one shot in fronta the Texaco station; who're we *kiddin'* here? Hey, I was O.K., but *you* got potential I *never* had.

Joey: But Itchy Halloran's *my height, DeSapio's* twice my *size*—

Eddie (*ignoring him*): O.K., first blow; your instinct is go for the belly, right?

Joey: *Instinct?* His belly is as high as I can *reach*, Pop—

Eddie: Wrong: first blow, forget the belly. Pointer Number One—ya listenin'?

Joey: Yeah.

Eddie (*demonstrating, precisely*): Considerin' the size, you gotta rock this boy *early* . . . gotta take the first one up from the *ground, vertical*, so your full body-weight's in the shot. Now, start of the fight, right away, *imm*ediate, you hunk *down*, move outa range; then *he's* gotta come to *you*—and you meet him with a right fist up *off the ground*; picture a spot in the middle of his chin and aim for it—*(demonstrates blow; Joey copies)* then comes the important part—

Joey: What's that?

Eddie: Jump back.

Joey: Jump back?

Eddie: Yeah, ya jump back so when he falls he don't hurt ya.

Joey: When he *falls*? *Murder*, he's gonna murder me. Pop, Pop, this is an *execution* I'm goin' to here! I'm only goin' so I won't be ashamed!

Eddie: There's only one thing you gotta watch out for—

Joey: *Death*, I gotta watch out for *death*—

Eddie: Not death . . . but there could be some damage. Could turn out to be more than one guy there, you're gettin' ganged up on, somethin' *special*—this *happens*, kid—O.K., we got a weapon here—*(takes framed photo of Boxer from wall)* we got a weapon here, guaranteed. *(Hands photo to Joey.)* What's it say there?

Joey *(reading)*: "Anybody gives *you* trouble, give *me* trouble. I love you. Love, Vince."

Eddie: O.K.; June Four, Nineteen Twenty-One, I come into the ring against Vince DiGangi, they bill him "The Ghetto Gorilla"—a shrimp with a mustache, nothin', I figure an easy win. Five *seconds* into Round One comes a *chamalia* from this little Eye-tie—I'm out, I'm on the canvas, your Pop is *furniture*, Joey. I open one eye, *there's* DiGangi on his knees next to me, he's got me in his arms, he's huggin' me, he's kissin' my face, he loves me. I give him his first big win, his first knockout. I *made* him, he says, he's gonna love me forever. And he *does*. That's the nice thing about these Telanas, they love ya or they hate ya, but it's forever; *so, remember—(leans towards him)* things get outa hand, you got a group situation, somethin'—you holler "DiGangi è mio fratello, *chiamalo!*" *(Grips his shoulder.)* "DiGangi è mio fratello, *chiamalo!*" Say it.

Joey: "DiGangi è mio fratello, chi . . . amalo!"

Eddie: That's "DiGangi's my brother, *call* him!" *(Softly, awestruck, imitating their response:)* Whoa . . . "DiGangi" 's the magic word down there, biggest hit since Columbus, lotta power with the mob. Perhaps you noticed, Big Vito don't come around here pushin' protection, whatever. This is the result of *one* word from Mr. Vincent DiGangi. *(Pats Joey's hand.)* Very heavy ticket there, kid, you don't want to use it unless the straits is completely dire. *(Slaps bar.)* O.K., ya got all that?

Joey *(starting towards front door without much spirit)*: Yeah; take the first one up from the ground, jump back, and tell 'em about DiGangi if I still got a mouth left. *(As he passes Stroller; softly, sighing:)* Well . . . here I go, Charlie.

Charlie *(speaking on behalf of the silent child)*: So long, Joey. Murder 'im.

(Joey stops at door; brushes off his shirt, stands up straighter, taller—then puts on his yarmulkeh.)

Eddie: What're ya doin' *that* for?

Joey: This'll drive 'im crazy. *(Flings open door, darts off into street, racing past Hannah Di Blindeh and Nick, a matching pair of ragged, aging alcoholics who have been standing in the threshold; they are early-morning drinkers who have clearly been waiting at the door for the bar to open, anxious for their first shot of the day. We hear Joey's voice as he races down the street.)* They're here, Pop.

Eddie *(looks up)*: Ah . . . Fred and Ginger. *(Checks pocket watch.)* Eight o'clock; on the button. Dance right in, kids.

Charlie *(gradually remembering, as they enter)*: Jesus, it's *them* . . . Of course, of *course* . . . no day could begin without them . . .

(Hannah, near sixty, Russian, and obviously sightless, wears faded, oddly elegant, overly mended clothing that may have been fashionable thirty years earlier. Nick's bushy white beard and matted hair make it hard to read his age, anywhere between early fifties and late sixties depending on the time of day; he has a soiled, ill-fitting suit and shirt, what had once been a tie, a noticeably red nose, and a clear case of the pre-first-drink shakes. During the minute or so of Charlie's next speech, Hannah, Nick and Eddie will go through the

very specific steps of their morning ritual. Before they reach their assigned bar-stools, Eddie will have dropped a piece of lemon peel into a stemmed glass, filled it halfway with cold vodka and placed it in front of one stool, then snapped a neat row of three shot-glasses down in front of the other, briskly filling each with straight bourbon. With due courtliness, Nick will escort Hannah to the bar, pull out her stool for her, not sit till she is seated; then she will finish her vodka in three separate delicate sips, saying "Lomir lebn un lachn" before each, while in exactly the same tempo, Nick says "You bet" in response to each of her toasts and downs his row of bourbon shots, his shakes vanishing with the contents of the third glass, Hannah finally sighing "Nit do gedacht" as she sets her empty glass down to end the first round; all this beginning and ending with the following speech, Charlie thoughtful, remembering, as he talks to us.)

Charlie: Hannah . . . Hannah Di Blindeh—meaning Hannah The Blind One; I used to think Di Blindeh was her last name—and Nick; I didn't know his last name, a problem he often shared with me till his third shot of bourbon—

Hannah: Lomir lebn un lachn—

Nick: You bet—

Charlie: Called "Nick" because, by his *sixth* shot, he believed—or would like *you* to believe, I was never sure which—that he was, in fact, Santa Claus; you can see the resemblance. In any case, this was an identity preferable to that of forcibly retired police sergeant; it seems that, in celebration of Repeal Day, Nick had managed to shoot out all the street-lamps in front of the Twenty-Second Precinct. He carried this famous Smith and Wesson with him every day to Pop's bar, which allowed them *both* to think of him as a kind of guard-bouncer for the place—God knows if he could still *aim* the damn thing, but Pop loved the street-lamp story and never charged him for a drink. Pop never charged Hannah for a drink either—

Hannah: Lomir lebn un lachn—

Charlie: That's "May we live and laugh."

Nick: You bet—

Charlie: She'd been blinded somehow on the second day of the October Pogrom; Hannah didn't remember what she saw that second day, but what she heard still woke her up every morning like an alarm clock—

Hannah: Lomir lebn un lachn—

Charlie: The noise didn't go away till she finished her first vodka.

Hannah (*sets her glass down*): Nit do gedacht.

Charlie: "May it never happen here."

Nick *(sets down his third shot-glass)*: You bet.

Hannah *(same Russian accent as Gusta, as she "looks" about)*: Something different here, Itzik. I got a feeling . . . no more "Frisco Eddie's."

Eddie: Right; I love ya, Hannah—it took *you* to notice.

Hannah: "Frisco Eddie's"—gone. This includes the Chuck-a-luck wheel, Eddie?

Nick: Yeah; he's got a kinda . . . museum here now.

Hannah: A shame; I *liked* that Chuck-a-luck wheel. But a museum, that's unusual. This could be something. The child, Eddie; he speaks yet?

Eddie: Well, fact is—

Hannah *(fondly)*: Vet meshiach geboyrn vern mit a tog shpeter.

Charlie: "So the Messiah will be born a day later."

Nick: You bet.

Hannah: Gentlemen—today's Number: I am considering seriously, at this time, betting Number Seven-Seven-Six; this in honor of Our Founding Fathers. Comments, please.

Nick: Seven-Seven-Six it *is*; a fine thought, Hannah.

Hannah: Next, we make the horse selections. You have brought the sheet, Nick?

Nick *(takes Racing Form from pocket)*: At the ready, darlin'.

Hannah: Excellent. *(As Nick escorts her to their table:)* Until such day, which is likely never, they make a Braille Racing Form, you and me is buddies, Nick.

Nick: Longer than that, sweetheart, longer than that . . .

(Finney The Book suddenly bursts into the room—a tight, tiny bundle of forty-five-year-old Irish nerves under a battered Fedora, he heads straight for his special upstage booth near the wall-phone. Usually anxious, depressed and fidgety, he seems in particularly bad shape today; the sound of Nineteen-Thirties Irish New York and the look of Greek tragedy.)

Eddie: Hey, Finney!

Nick: Mornin', Finn'.

Charlie *(fondly, as Finney enters booth)*: Ah, Finney . . . our Bookmaker In Residence; Finney The Book arrives at his office, ready to take bets on the Daily Number, and an occasional horse—early today but tragic as ever, having given up on the Irish Rebellion twenty years ago for a cause with even worse odds . . .

Finney (*slumps in booth*): Oh, me friends . . . me friends . . . Nick, Eddie, Hannah . . . truly the Tsouris is on me this day!

Hannah: Finney, darling . . . what *is* it?

Finney: What is it? What *is* it, y' say? It's the bloody July *Fourth*, is what it is! Every bloody Greenhorn from here to the river bettin' Seven-Seven-Six, every bloody Guinea, Mick, Jew and China-boy bettin' the Independence! (*Rising solemnly in his booth.*) "Finney, Finney," I say to m'self the dawn of every Fourth. "Finney, m'boy, stay in your *bed* this cursed and twisted day!"—and *fool* that I am, *ob*liged as I am t'me regulars, I hit the bloody *street*! It's me damned code of *honor* does me in! (*Shoves his hands deep into the pockets of his baggy suit-jacket—we hear now the jingle and rustle of hundreds of quarters in one and hundreds of singles in the other.*) Four *hundred*—four hundred *easy* on Seven-Seven-Six and the mornin' still new yet! Seven-Seven-Six comes in, me entire Mishpocheh's eatin' *toast* for a year! (*Suddenly aware of the dozens of American flags about him.*) And what have ya got *here*, Eddie, me bloody *funeral* arrangements?! My God, man, the only thing missin's a bloody fife and drum to march me to me grave!

Nick (*pointing to phone*): Well, you'd best start layin' off some bets then, Thomas—

Finney: Every damn Book in the *city's* tryin' to lay off the same bloody number, boy! Tom Finney, what's to *become* of ya? Finney, Finney . . . *(Suddenly turns to Eddie.)* And while we're on it, Edward—even I do survive this day—I can't be givin' ya no more twenty for the use o' me booth; it's ten at best, here on.

Eddie: What *is* this, *lep*rechaun humor? *(To Hannah and Nick:)* Man's kiddin' me, right?—his own booth, his own personal *booth* Nine till Post Time, *choice* location—

Finney: Edward, Edward, all me fondness, ya know damn well I'm bringin' in more pony-people who drink than you're bringin' in drinkers who'll wager—*(Indicates Stroller.)* Eight-to-one the boy don't say a word till Christmas. *(Heads briskly to phone.)*

Eddie: The new *place*, I'm *tellin'* ya, it's all gonna turn around—

Finney *(grabs phone)*: Better start layin' off now or I'm surely gornisht in the mornin'. *(Dialing anxiously.)* Home of the bloody *brave* . . .

Hannah *(handing quarter out towards him)*: Finney, darling: twenty-five cents on number Seven-Seven-Seven. May you live and be well.

Finney *(takes coin)*: Blessin's on ya—*(Into phone:)* Ah, now, is that me sweet Bernie there, the Saint Bernard himself? Finney here, and wonderin' would you care to take two hundred on—*(to the dead phone in his hand)* Star-Spangled bloody Banner . . . *(Dialing* *again.)* Finney, Finney, you're sendin' an S.O.S. to a fleet o' sinkin' ships . . .

(He will continue, quietly, to call several more "Banks" through this next scene; the following dialogue between Nick and Hannah will happen at the same time as his call to Bernie.)

Nick *(opens Racing Form)*: Where ya want to start: Belmont, Thistledown, Arlington Park . . . ?

Hannah: I say Thistledown; why not?

Nick: Thistledown it *is* then. O.K., first race we got Dancin' Lady, four-year-old filly, Harvest Moon by Wild Time, carryin' one fifteen . . .

(They will continue, quietly and with great concentration, to pick horses for the next several minutes—both Finney's call to Bernie and their above dialogue happening at the same time as the entrance of two new customers: Blue, followed a few moments later by Jimmy Scalso. Blue is large, Irish, about fifty, slow-moving, powerful, seeming at all times vaguely amused either by something that happened some time ago or something that might happen soon.)

Blue *(taps bar)*: You got Johnny Red?

Eddie *(pouring drink)*: Like the choice; *I* got it— *(Snaps it on bar.)* Now *you* got it.

(Jimmy Scalso enters a few moments later, sleekly Italian, just thirty, wiry, a smiler, wearing the kind of carefully tailored silk suit that demands a silver crucifix on a chain about his neck; he speaks and moves rapidly and surely but is still somehow auditioning for a role he hasn't gotten yet. Scalso steps jauntily up to the bar, sits on a stool near Nick and Hannah; Blue takes his drink to a distant table, opens his newspaper.)

Scalso: You got Daitch on tap, fellah?

Eddie: I got it; like the choice. *(Working tap-spigot.)* I got it—*(Places full mug on bar.)* Now *you* got it.

Scalso: New place, huh? I see the sign outside, "Opening Day." *(Eddie nods pleasantly.)* I like the feel. Lotta wood; none of that chrome shit, shiny shit. And the lights: not dark, just . . . soft; like it's always, what? Evening here. *(Pause; sips his beer.)* So here we are, the *both* of us, huh?—workin' on a holiday. Ain't been on a vacation, when?—three, no four, *four* years ago. Four years ago, February. I take the wife and the kid to Miami. O.K., sand, sun, surf; *one* day, it's *over* for me, enough. I'm the kinda guy—

Nick *(to Scalso, quietly)*: Do you know who I am?

Scalso *(ignoring him like the barfly he is)*: —kinda guy I am, I don't get the *point* of a vacation. You go, you come back, there you *are* again. I'm the kinda guy, I gotta be movin', workin'.

Hannah: Give him a hint, Nick.

Nick: I give you a hint; "Ho, ho, ho."

Scalso: They say, what?—"don't mix business with pleasure," right? Well, business *is* my pleasure, what can I tell ya? Second day in Miami, second *day*, I'm goin' crazy, I wanna get *outa* there.

Nick (*speaking confidentially, to Scalso*): You better watch out . . . you better not cry; better not pout, I'm tellin' you why . . .

Scalso: Here in town, I'm up, a cup of coffee, a little juice, I'm outa the house—I can't *wait* to go to work. Saturday, *Sun*day, I don't *give* a shit. The wife says to me, "Jimmy, Sunday, we'll go to the park; you, me, the kid, we row a boat." I says to her, "Baby, I hate that shit, I'm *not* that kinda *guy*." She says—

Eddie (*leans towards him, quietly*): Would you do something for me?

Scalso: What?

Eddie: Shut the hell up.

Scalso: Huh?

Eddie: Shut your goddamn face. Zip it up. Can it. Button the ruby-reds. Silencio. Got it?

Scalso: Hey, Mister, what the hell kinda—?

Eddie: You're boring. I can't stand it. It's killin' me. That Moose up there, he's dead, it don't bother him. Me, while you're talkin' I got individual brain cells up here dyin' one at a time. Two minutes with you, I'm sayin' Kaddish for my brain. Shut up and drink your beer.

Nick (*confidentially, to Scalso*): I'm makin' a list . . . and checkin' it twice, gonna find out who's naughty and nice . . .

Scalso: How come ya got a guy here half off his *nut*, and *I'm* the one ya—?

Eddie: Because who he *thinks* he is is a hundred times more interestin' than who you *are*. You ain't just borin', buddy, you're a goddamn *pioneer* in the field.

Scalso: Hey, I come in here for a beer, a little conversation, I don't expect a guy to—

Eddie: You think the price of a beer you own *one minute* of my time? (*Leans close to him; calmly:*) O.K., I got two things I want ya to do for me. The first thing I want ya to do is go away, and the next thing I want ya to do is never come back. That's two things; can ya remember that?

Scalso *(slaps bar)*: Place is open to the public, I got a right to sit here and drink my beer. Who you *oughta* be throwin' out is these two *drunks* here—

Eddie: I got a private club here, pal. I got my own rules. You just had a free beer; goodbye.

Scalso: This ain't no private club.

Eddie *(indicating bar-room)*: Right, this ain't no private club; but this—*(takes billy-club out from under bar; grips it firmly)* this is a private club. It's called the Billy Club. Billy is the president. He wants you to leave.

(Hannah raises her head, listening; Blue looks up from his newspaper; Finney turns from the phone, watching, tensely twisting his hat.)

Scalso *(after a moment)*: Ya mean you're willin' to beat the shit outa some guy just because ya think he's *borin'*?

Eddie *(taps the club)*: Right; self-*defense*, pal.

(Scalso suddenly starts to laugh, slapping the bar, enjoying himself.)

Blue *(puts his drink down)*: Come on, Jimmy; tell him, we got a long day comin'.

Scalso: Hey, Blue, Blue, I like this guy, I like this guy
. . . *I like this guy! (Still laughing; Eddie regarding
him stonily, tightening grip on club.)* You are *great*,
Goldberg . . . you are *some*thin', baby . . . "A private
club, the *Billy* Club" . . . great, great . . .

Blue *(rising from table, impatient with him)*: Enough
now; we got alotta *work* here, boy.

Scalso *(still chuckling)*: Absolutely right, babe. Goldberg . . . Goldberg, Goldberg, *Goldberg*; you are cute,
you are some cute Jew, you are the cutest Jew I ever
saw. And tough; I never seen such a tough Jew, I include the Williamsburg Boys. *(Eddie, his club at the
ready, waiting him out.)* I'm Jimmy Scalso; maybe you
don't hear, various internal problems, Vito had an ap-
pointment with the Hudson River, which he kept, Seranno gimme alla his Stops; bye-bye, Big Vito—bon
jour, Jimmy. *(Eddie, absorbing this, lowers club to his
side.)* Y'know, I seen ya box, barkeep, Stauch's Arena,
I'm sixteen—hey, Blue, this was *some*thin', The East
Side Savage against Ah Soong, The Fightin' China-
man—

Blue: Move it along, boy; move it *along*, will ya?

Scalso: Absolutely right, babe. O.K., business, Goldberg; Vito's got fifty-four Stops, fifty-three is solid—
some reason he lets one of 'em slide; yours. I'm checkin'
the books, ya got no cigarette machine here, ya don't
got our *Defense* System, you got a Box should be doin'
two and a half a month, you're doin' seventy. *Our* rec-

ords, selected *hits, thirty* top tunes a month—you take only *two. (Points to Jukebox.)* Blue, what's he *got* on there? *(Slaps himself on the head.)* Shit, where's my goddamn *manners*—Mr. Goldberg, this is Blue, for Blue-Jaw McCann; called such because the man could shave five times a day, he's still got a jaw turns gunmetal blue by evenin', same color as the fine weapon he carries. A man, in his prime, done hench for Amato, Scalisi, Carafano . . .

(Scalso pauses a moment, letting this sink in. Eddie puts his club down on the bar. Scalso nods, acknowledging Eddie's good sense.)

Blue *(checking the Jukebox)*: All right, he's got eight here by a fella, Leba—Leba—

Hannah: *Lebedeff.* Aaron Lebedeff, the Maurice Chevalier of the Jewish Stage—

Blue: Then there's a couple, a fella, Zatz, half-a-dozen Eddie Cantor, somebody Ukelele Ike, Jolson, Kate Smith, The U.S. Army Band, Irish Eyes—

Scalso *(his head in his hands)*: Stop, stop, stop, *night*mare, it's a *night*mare! Somebody *wake* me, I'm *dreamin*'! Goldberg, Goldberg, you're takin' the joie outa my goddamn *vie* here! *(Looks up mournfully, shouting:)* Whatta ya think ya *got* here, Goldberg, a *Victrola?* This is a *Box,* this is *our* goddamn *Box* here, *income, income.* Weird foreign shit, hundred-year-old *losers,* and mosta the plays is your own *slugs*! Where's the *hits*, where's—*(Stops himself; quietly:)* O.K., everybody calm down. A new day, a new dollar, right? *(Pacing, to Blue:)* No Butts, no Defense, shit on the Box; Vito musta been crazy . . .

Finney *(whispering)*: Tell him, Eddie; DiGangi . . .

Eddie *(whispering, sharply)*: Shut up.

Scalso *(pleasantly, a man bestowing gifts)*: O.K., new deal, we start fresh—my true belief: everybody's happy. Goldberg, item one, comes tomorrow, A.M., cigarette machine—fifty-fifty split; Butts come certain sources, the price is hilarious. Item two: Angelo Defense System—I hear ya screamin': "Protection racket, ugly Italian behavior, get me outa here!" *(Softly, almost misty-eyed:)* My reply: au *contraire*, my darlin' Hebrew, a Wop and a Yid is one heart beatin' here. "Angelo Defense System": meanin' defense against every greasy hand wants *in* your satchel! The cops *alone*, whatta ya pay Christmas? Also Inspectors: Fire, Garbage, whatever—the Angel flies in. Figure what you save, one monthly shot to the Angel; words fail. *(Crossing up to Jukebox.)* The Box; tomorrow, A.M., my people come, *out* goes the goddamn funeral music, the Memory Lane Losers, the Hollerin' Hebes—*in* comes forty selected hits; once-a-week collection. Finney here, business as usual; already under the wing, a Defense System who I'm affiliated. *Finale*: same split like Vito on the Box, *plus* you got a one G advance from me on your end, good will, get acquainted, my pocket to yours, this very day. *(Strides back down to bar, takes* *neatly folded wad of hundreds from jacket, places it on bar in front of the silent Eddie, sits on stool opposite him; then flatly, evenly:)* Now, some banana-nut reason, this deal don't appeal; need I mention, things happen. The Angel come down, fly away with the Liquor License, twenty, thirty days, outa business. Things break, toilets don't work, beer deliveries slow down— *(Suddenly smacks himself on the forehead.)* What the hell am I talkin'!? I gotta tell The East Side Savage birds-and-bees basics? You know the story. Gimme the Brocheh, baby; we go in peace. Whatta ya say?

(Silence; he waits for Eddie's answer as does everyone else in the barroom. A thoughtful moment, then Eddie picks up the wad of bills.)

Eddie *(turns to Hannah, quietly)*: Hannah, how about you take Charlie into the kitchen, give him a little something to eat. Brisket's on your right, some Lokshen on the left. *(Hannah, with some help from Nick, wheels the Stroller into the Kitchen and exits as Eddie turns to Scalso, continuing pleasantly:)* Fact of the matter, you first come in here, I figure you are definitely not with the Salvation Army; and this guy here, the bulge in the right jacket-pocket is probably not his Holy Bible, I say to myself. *(Blue chuckles softly, Scalso smiles.)* I do *not* know you are a Seranno boy, got alla Vito's Stops now. *(He shrugs apologetically.)* Not knowin' this, I do the club thing for ya, kinda demonstrate my attitude and feelings how I run my place. *(A beat; then he tosses the wad of bills into Scalso's lap.)* Which remains the exact same. You're boring me to death, Ginzo. *(Continues calmly:)* I want your nose and your ass, and everything you got in between, *outa* my business. I don't want your cigarette machine, your records, your advice, and I want your goddamn Angel off my shoulder. I give you the same deal I give Vito on the Box, and that's *it*. And now I want you and your over-the-hill hench outa my joint instantaneous. Goodbye and good luck. *(He picks up the club, raps it sharply on the bar like a gavel.)* Conversation over; end of conversation.

(Scalso remains quite still, Blue takes a small step forward from the Jukebox, Charlie rises tensely in his booth, Finney is wringing his Fedora like a wet bathing suit.)

Hannah's Voice *(softly, from Kitchen)*: Pogrom . . . pogrom . . . pogrom . . .

Scalso *(points to his silver crucifix; quietly)*: This here J.C., my Pop give it to me; remind me of Our Savior, but mostly, he says, to do things peaceful before I do 'em hard; this has been my approach with you here. But you know what comes to me, I listen to you? Sooner or later, tough or chicken, lucky, unlucky, Jews is Jews. Ain't this the way, Blue? Ain't this the way? Goddamn *guests* in this country, they are—they're here ten minutes, they're tellin' ya how to *run* the place . . . *(He puts his hand on Eddie's arm.)* I pride myself, makin' friends with you Jews—but sooner or later, every *one* of ya—

(Eddie reaches forward, gets a firm grip on Scalso's crucifix and chain and pulls him across the bar with it, holding him firmly down on the bar.)

Eddie: You was holdin' my arm . . .

Scalso *(struggling)*: Hey, my J.C., my J.C.—

Eddie: You know us Jews, we can't keep our hands off the guy.

Scalso: *Blue, Blue . . .*

(Blue thrusts his hand into his gun-pocket, Nick turns to him; Finney races up stairs, hovering in Apartment doorway.)

Eddie *(retaining firm grip on Scalso)*: Here's the situation: Mr. Blue, whatever you got in mind right now, a fact for ya: Nick here, an ex-cop, got two friends with him, Mr. Smith and Mr. Wesson; there's some say his aim ain't what it used to be, but a target your size he's bound to put a hole in it somewhere; 'sides which, he don't care if he kills ya, he thinks Donder an' Blitzen gonna take the rap for him anyway. *(Lets go of Scalso, holds his billy-club high in the air; all in the room frozen.)* Scalso, any part of you makes a move on me, I bust it with Billy. This is the situation, both of ya. Stay and make a move; or go. *(Moving up to Jukebox, watching them carefully.)* Meantime, while you're makin' up your mind, I got a need to hear one o' those Hollerin' Hebes; gonna play one of my records on my Box here

. . . *(Quickly deposits slug, makes selection; turns to face them, his club at the ready.)* My personal suggestion, we go for a safe and sane Fourth.

(Eddie's eyes dart from Scalso to Blue, Finney grips the edge of the Apartment doorway; Blue, his hand firmly in his gun-pocket, looks over at Nick, sizing him up. Nick, still standing at the far end of the bar, slips his hand into the holster under his jacket, holds it there.)

Nick *(quietly, to Blue)*: I see you when you're sleepin', I know when you're awake; I know if you've been bad or good, so be good for goodness sake . . .

Finney *(whispering urgently to Eddie)*: Just tell 'em about DiGangi; we stop all this, Eddie—

Eddie *(quietly)*: Don't need him, I got it under control. This is *mine*.

(Suddenly, from the Jukebox, we begin to hear Aaron Lebedeff's rousing rendition of "In Odessa" and its irresistibly danceable Klezmer Band backup; Lebedeff sings a dream of the old Moldavanka, inviting us to return to a world of swirling skirts, endless dancing, grand times till dawn in the shoreline cafés of the Black Sea and, of course, the food that was served there. Nick, Scalso, Finney, Blue and Charlie remaining quite still, the pulsing beat of the Klezmer Band filling the silence of this tense moment, Eddie starting to snap the fingers of his left hand to the beat, the billy-club still held high

in his right, Music continuing to build through the scene.)

Lebedeff's Voice:
"In Ades, in Ades, af der Moldavanke,
Tantst men dort a Palanez, mit a sheyn tsiganke . . ."

(Scalso rises suddenly from his barstool, going to center of room, forceful, commanding, on top of it again.)

Scalso *(shouting, pointing fiercely at Eddie)*: The man *marked* me, Blue; he put a *mark* on me! *(Blue takes a step forward; Scalso clenches his fists, ready to spring.)* O.K., school's in *session* now, barkeep; *lesson* time; Professor Blue and me, we gonna *teach* you something . . .

Joey's Voice *(shouting, from street)*: Pop! Hey, *Pop!*

(Zaretsky suddenly bursts through the front door, his arm around a somewhat battered, bloody-nosed, but very proud Joey. A man who knows how to make an entrance, Zaretsky speaks immediately as he comes through the door, using the threshold as his stage; the Group remains frozen.)

Zaretsky: No, not since David and Goliath have I seen such! Yes, the child bleeds, but wait till you see what this *DeSapio* looks like—

Joey: He went *down*, Pop, he went *down*—*(Indicating his bloody nose.)* I mean, later he got *up*, but there was—

Zaretsky: Please, Jussel, allow me—I come upon this child, familiar to me at a distance; opposing him, I tell you, a veritable *Visigoth* of a boy, he—*(His voice trails off; he becomes aware of the stillness in the room.)* I feel that I do not have the full attention of this group.

Eddie *(quickly, quietly)*: Congratulations, kid. Go to Sussman's, pick up the bread order. Now.

Joey: Pop, I gotta tell ya—

Eddie: *Suss*man's. *Now.*

Joey: Christ's sake, Pop—

Eddie: *Now!*

Joey *(as he reluctantly exits)*: Christ's sake . . .

(Zaretsky sees the billy-club in Eddie's hand, glances at the unfamiliar figures of Scalso and Blue; Eddie remaining quite still, snapping his fingers as the Music continues, swaying slightly to the beat.)

Eddie: Anton, we got a situation here.

Scalso *(grips Blue's arm, urgently)*: Now, Blue, *now*; place is fillin' up. Look, Blue, man wants to dance; help him dance, Blue—the feet, go for the feet. I want to see the man *dance*, make him dance, make him *nervous* . . .

Blue *(after a moment; his eyes fixed on Eddie)*: Nervous? You ain't gonna make *this* boy nervous. This boy don't *get* nervous; which is what's gonna kill him one fine day. *(Pulls his empty hand sharply out of his gunpocket, his gaze never leaving Nick and Eddie.)* Now *today*, Jimmy, here's how the cards lay down: what you got here is an ol' shithouse and a crazy Jew. Two and a half on this Box, boy? You give this Jew Bing Crosby in person, you give him Guy Lombardo appearin' nightly, he don't pull in more'n a hundred. Now, tell me, Jimmy-Boy, you want me to go shoot Santa Claus for a hundred-dollar Box?

Scalso *(urgently, commanding)*: We gotta leave a *mark*, Blue, on *some*body, on *some*thing. Fifty-four Stops, this news travels; there gotta be *consequences* here, Blue, things *happened* here—

Blue: *Consequences*? This Jew don't know consequences and don't care. Look at his eyes, Jimmy. He just wants to kill you, boy; don't care if he dies the next minute, and don't care who dies with him. Make it a rule, Jimmy-Boy, you don't want to get into a fight, weapon or no, with a man ain't lookin' to live. *(He turns, walks briskly towards front door.)*

Scalso *(not moving, rubbing neck-burn)*: Things *happened* here, Blue—

Blue: Seranno ain't gonna give a cobbler's crap about this place—fifty-three Stops to *cover*, Jimmy-Boy, let's go.

Scalso *(silence for a moment; then, striding angrily towards Blue)*: Hey, hey—how about you leave off callin' me "Jimmy-Boy," huh? How about we quit that shit, right?

Blue *(patting Scalso's shoulder)*: In the old Saint Pat's, y'know, over on Prince, we used t'make you Guineas have mass in the basement. Biggest mistake we ever made was lettin' you boys up on the first floor. *(He exits. Scalso remains in doorway, turns towards Eddie.)*

Scalso *(pointing, fiercely)*: O.K., now here's somethin' for *you* and *Billy* and the entire fuckin' *club*—

(But the Lebedeff Music has built to an irresistible Freylekeh rhythm—irresistible, that is, to any triumphant Jew in the room—and Eddie, holding the billy-club over his head with both hands, begins to spin around the center table to the beat.)

Eddie: Hey, Jimmy-Boy, you wanted to see the man dance . . . he's dancin' . . . *(Takes his handkerchief out of his pocket, extends it towards Zaretsky, a gesture of invitation as old as the Music he dances to.)* Hey, Actor, Actor . . . come, come, this Ginzo loves dancin' . . .

(Zaretsky joins Eddie in perhaps the only thing they can ever agree upon, the pleasure of dancing to an old Lebedeff tune; Zaretsky takes the other end of the handkerchief and, the handkerchief held taut between them over their heads, they dance aggressively towards Scalso, their feet stomping to the beat, Scalso backing away towards the door. Joey suddenly bursts through the door just behind Scalso, shouting at his back.)

Joey: DiGangi! DiGangi è mio fratello! Chiamalo! Chiamalo!

Scalso *(surrounded by two dancing Jews and a screaming child; he shouts)*: Buncha crazy Hebes here . . . !

(Scalso exits into the street. Zaretsky and Eddie triumphant, Zaretsky swirling to the Music, Eddie beating out the rhythm fiercely with his club, Finney and Nick clapping to the beat, Joey's arms in the air, shouting.)

Joey: It *works*, Pop! The Di*Gangi* number; it works! It works!

Eddie: Of *course* it works!

Joey *(proudly)*: *Comes* to me, Pop, comes to me these guys don't *look* right, see—

Eddie: Nobody messes with the Ross boys!

Joey: Who?

Eddie: Ross! Ross! Joey *Ross*—the kid who beat DeSapio!

Joey: But I didn't *win*, Pop—

Eddie *(prowling the room with his club, his tension unreleased by Scalso's defeat)*: *Sure* you won, kid, we only got winners here, *winners* . . .

Zaretsky *(points a challenging finger)*: So then, Itzik, I have seen you rise from your knees—something of your spirit has been touched today!

Eddie *(fiercely)*: Only thing got touched was my goddamn *arm*, Actor.

Hannah *(leaning out of kitchen)*: So, the coast, I am assuming, is clear?

Eddie: Everything under control here, babe.

Hannah *(standing in kitchen doorway)*: Gentlemen . . . I got big news . . .

Zaretsky: What, Hannah?

Hannah: Gentlemen . . . *the child has spoken*!

(The Group cheers, but Eddie cuts sharply through them.)

Eddie: *What?* What did he say . . . ?

(All fix on Hannah expectantly as Nick guides her down into the room.)

Hannah: Two statements, clear like a bell. The first, very nice, he touches my hand, he says, "Papa." *(All but Eddie responding happily; he remains silent, quite still.)* The second statement, a little embarrassing to repeat . . .

Eddie: *What*, Hannah . . . ?

Hannah: A couple seconds later, he's got my hand again, this time a firm grip, he says—clear like a bell, I tell you—"No shit from nobody!"

(Zaretsky applauds lustily, shouting "Bravo," Nick and Finney cheer loudly, waving their hats, Joey leaps joyously in the air yelling "Hey, Champ"; Eddie remains silent, striding sharply away from the cheering Group, his club held tight in his fist.)

Eddie *(shouting, fiercely, above the Group)*: And no exceptions . . . ! *(Raising club violently over his head.)* No exceptions . . . nobody . . . ! *(smashing club down on center table)* nobody . . . !

(The Group turns to him, startled, quite still, as Eddie continues, out of control now, wildly, striking a chair, another table, killing them like Cossacks, shouting with each blow.)

Eddie: . . . *nobody . . . nobody . . . (Striking Charlie's booth, Charlie rising to his feet, riveted.) Nobody! . . . (Eddie freezes with this last shout, his club held high in the air, ready to strike another blow as . . .)*

THE CURTAIN FALLS

ACT
TWO

Before the curtain rises we hear a full Chorus and Marching Band moving up into a thunderous, rousing, next-to-last stanza of "Columbia, the Gem of the Ocean."

Chorus:

"Three cheers for the red, white and blue,
Three cheers for the red, white and blue,
The Army and Navy forever,
Three cheers for the red, white and blue . . ."

At Rise: *The blaring trumpets rise in pitch to herald the final stanza as the curtain goes up. Charlie alone in the darkened bar—the dim, early evening light of the Present—seated exactly where he was at the beginning of the play, at the far end of the bar near the glowing Jukebox, listening thoughtfully to the triumphant conclusion of the Music to which Eddie first burst into the room.*

Chorus:

"Three cheers for the red, white and blue,
Three cheers for the red, white and blue,
Thy banners make tyranny tremble,
Three cheers for the red, white and blue . . ."

A cymbal-crashing, drum-rolling finale; Charlie con-tinues to look into the colors of the now silent Jukebox for a moment or two, then turns to us.

Charlie: *(indicating Moose)*: Well—as Morris will tell you—the Golden Door Tavern did *not* get us Uptown; nor did Eddie Ross' Silver Horseshoe, the Empire State Sports Club, or even Ed Ross' Riverview, mostly because we didn't have one. *(Inserting slug in Jukebox, making selection.)* But then came the summer of Forty-Four, the heyday of Café Society and, of course, its pulsating heart—Sherman Billingsley's Stork Club. *(With a sweeping gesture towards bar.)* Eddie's response was swift and glorious: Ladies and Gentleman, July Third, Nineteen Forty-Four . . . the Opening Day of the Flamingo Lounge.

(A huge pink and crimson plaster-and-glass chandelier in the shape of a flamingo in flight—its spread wings, thrust-back legs and proudly arched head framed by several dozen glowing pink light bulbs—descends through the ceiling over the bar as we begin to hear the catchy bongo and trumpet Calypso intro to the Andrews Sisters' recording of "Rum and Coca-Cola" coming from the Jukebox.)

Andrews Sisters:
　"Out on Mandenella Beach,
　G.I. romance with native peach,
　All day long make tropic love,
　Next day sit in hot sun and cool off, drinkin'—
　Rum and Coca-Cola . . ."

(Music continuing, building, as lights come up full; it's exactly eight years later, about 7 A.M. on Monday, July 3, 1944, and we see that the bar-room has gone through a transition from general Early American to general Tropical Caribbean, the dominant theme, as always, being Gin-Mill Shabby. The Early American stuff remains but joining it now are coconut-shell candle holders and plastic pineapples on each table, crepe-paper leis hung about on hooks, an incandescent tropical-sunset painting over the Jukebox, brightly illustrated placards announcing various rum-punch drinks and their "Reasonable Introductory Prices" tacked up on the walls, running across the bottom of the mirror a red and white banner reading "Welcome to the Flamingo! Opening Day!" and over the door a painting of a flamingo with just the word "Lounge" under it. Eddie's usual Fourth of July bunting across the top of the mirror and small flags along the bar are in evidence, though the flags have not yet been put on the tables and booths. In addition, it is the summer of the Fifth Annual "Miss Daitch" Contest and a string of six small posters, featuring a smiling head-shot and brief bio of each Contestant, hangs across the right wall just above the booths; beneath these a bright banner states the Daitch Beer slogan: "There Is a Difference and the Difference Is Daitch"; below that: "Vote Here for Miss Daitch, 1944," and next to the far right booth a ballot-box and a stack of ballots. All this revealed as the Music and Charlie continue.)

Charlie: And tonight . . . the Victory Party, in honor of what we're all sure will be Joey's twenty-eighth straight win since he got his Amateur Card . . . *(as Joey, almost eighteen now, enters from the Kitchen with a tray of plastic pineapples, places them on tables, his boxer's authority and the tiptoe bounce of his walk distinctly similar to his father's)* . . . twenty-three knockouts, six in the first three rounds, and four decisions. Got his A.A.U. card at fourteen—two years before the legal age—by using Vince DiGangi's son Peter's Baptism Certificate, so he's earned a very big reputation over the last four years for somebody called Pistol Pete DiGangi. *(Joey turns, heading up to bar, the back of his jacket emblazoned with a "Pistol Pete" logo.)* I, of course, was known as the only kid ever to be knocked down by Cock-Eye Celestini—he being several years my junior, an infant really, and visually disabled—

Eddie *(bursts in from the Kitchen, delighted, waving a folded newspaper)*: Hey, ya see the ad in the "Mirror" this morning?—ya see that?—top of the *Card* tonight, Joey, top of the *Card*. "Bazooka-Boy" Kilbane, *no*body —goddamn *Main Event* even *with* this Mick bozo! This is because ya made a goddamn *name* for yourself, kid! *(He moves over to Joey, the two sparring, jabbing, ducking, weaving about amidst the tables now, clearly a morning ritual, as Eddie continues.)* Let me tell ya about Kilbane's weak spot—his *body*; his entire body. Tonight's *pointer*? Bring some stamps with ya and *mail* the putz home! *(Indicates radio as their sparring continues.)* Broadcast—broadcast over the goddamn *air*waves tonight, Speed Spector him*self* doin' the

Blow-by-Blow; *Spector.* Closin' the place up soon as the fights start, nobody in here unless by special invite; victory party, champagne, the works. I'd be at ringside, per usual, but I gotta hear this comin' outa the *Philco*, kid, I *gotta.* After, Spector always does an On-the-Spot with the Main Event Winner; gotta *hear* it, right? *(As their sparring ends, Eddie—clearly outboxed and happily exhausted by Joey—returning to set up bar.)* By the way, durin' the On-the-Spot, ya wanna drop a mention there's a new class place openin' on Canal, the Flamingo Lounge, this is optional—*(Suddenly slaps his head.)* Will you shut ya *trap*, Eddie?! This is *your* night, kid—don't *mention* me—what the hell am I *talkin'* about?! Would somebody *please* tell me to shut *up*?!

Zaretsky *(entering from Apartment)*: All right; shut up. *(Moving down to his usual table, folding back page of newspaper.)* For all assembled, I have here a certain item . . .

Eddie: Shit, the Jew News . . .

Zaretsky: Gentlemen, we have here on page twelve of "The New York Times," amidst ads for Stern's Department Store and a Jewelry Consultant, an item, five sentences in length, which reports to us that four hundred thousand Hungarian Jews have thus far perished in the German death camps of Poland as of June Seventeenth; and further, that three hundred and fifty thousand more are presently being deported to Poland where they are expected to be put to death by July Twenty-Fourth. *This* on page twelve; however—*(turns to first page)* we find here on the front page of this same journal, a bold headline concerning today's holiday traffic; I quote: "Rail and Bus Travel Will Set New July Fourth Peak." *(Neatly folding paper.)* I offer these items, fellow residents, for the news itself, also an insight into the ironic editorial policies of America's most prominent daily journal; owned, incidentally, by Jews.

(Joey has moved down to Zaretsky's table, clearly absorbed, as always, by Zaretsky's "Jew News.")

Joey: *(quietly, studying newspaper)*: Jesus, the next three weeks . . . that's three hundred and fifty thousand in the next three *weeks* . . .

Eddie *(turns sharply from his work behind the bar)*: Come on, Actor, the *truth*—what's it *say* there? That's another one o' those "Informed Sources *say*," "Foreign Authorities *tell* us" goddamn stories, ain't it? If it's true, where's the *pictures*?! How come I never seen it in "Life" magazine? How come I never seen it in the "March of *Time*," they got *everything*! *Winchell* even! How come *Roosevelt* don't mention—if F.D.R. *believed* all that he'd be doin' somethin' about it this *minute, guaranteed*!

Zaretsky *(rising at his table)*: Itzik, you are a foolish tender of *bars*! *Election* year, he's *got* your vote al-

ready, he will not stir the *pot*! He will be silent, your
Golden Goy. He listens, he hears the old and horrible
songs—he knows that nobody believes the Jews are
dying, only that somehow Jews are making millions
from the war and want it. He will be quiet, Itzik, as
quiet now as the Jews of page twelve!

Eddie *(shouting)*: Do ya *mind*, Zaretsky? Do ya *mind*
if we just let the guy go and win the goddamn *war*? Is
that *O.K.* with you? The man knows what he's *doin'*,
pal—he does *now*, he always *did*, and he always *will*.
Meanwhile, you breathe one *word* of that crazy shit
durin' Joey's party and you're gonna see *my* twelve-
minute version of "The Dybbuk"!

Zaretsky *(slams his fist on the table)*: I *refuse*—I refuse, sir, to have a conversation of this nature with a
man who has just spent the morning putting light
bulbs in a huge pink bird! *(Turns to Joey, suddenly
pleasant, cordial; one of those instant transitions of
which this old actor is very fond.)* I am off then to the
home of the Widow Rosewald, who, among other favors, now repairs my robes for Lear, and kindly tol-
erates the aging process, both hers and mine. And, of
course, my best with the Bazooka tonight. Bonne
chance, Jussel, Joey, Goldberg, Ross, DiGangi—*(patting his cheek)* whoever you are. *(Striding to the front
door.)* Don't worry, Itzik; tonight I shall sit quietly and
cheer appropriately. In future, also, you will have less
concern of my Jew News . . . as there are fewer and

fewer Jews, there will be less and less news. *(He exits abruptly.)*

(Silence for a moment; Eddie continues busily setting up behind the bar, Joey studies the newspaper article, Charlie absorbed, watching all this from near the Juke-box and not his usual booth.)

Joey *(quietly)*: I think it's all true, Pop.

Eddie *(distracted)*: What?

Joey: What Mr. Zaretsky's tellin' us, Pop, I think it's all true. It's *gotta* be—I mean, look at all the shit that's goin' on *here*.

Eddie: Here is business as usual; maybe a little worse this summer.

Joey: A little *worse* this summer?—*(Moving down towards him.)* Pop, *Brooklyn*, they hit two cemeteries in one *week*. You been on Rivington lately?—Jewish stars with Swastikas painted over 'em, they're poppin' up on the walls like Lucky *Strike* ads. The Gladiators, the Avengers—*Boys'* clubs, they call 'em—they're on the prowl every night beatin' the crap outa Hebrew School kids. Grabbed a kid comin' outa Beth-El Saturday, ripped off his shirt and painted "Jew" on his chest, like maybe he *forgot*—you *hearin'* any of this, Pop?

Eddie *(busily stacking glasses, his back to Joey)*: It's not I ain't hearin' ya, kid; it's I *heard* it all already;

been goin' on since before you was born. But this stuff *Zaretsky*'s talkin' about—not even in the old Molda-vanka was there ever such.

Joey: But if it's true—

Eddie: If it's true then Uncle Nick's got his *sleigh* parked outside! It's all too crazy, kid, I'm tellin' ya. *(Turns to him.)* Now lemme *alone*, will ya—I gotta *open* here in twenty minutes! *(Joey moving thoughtfully up towards phone, Eddie glancing about.)* Shit, he ain't done the *set*-ups yet—*(Shouting:)* Charlie! Charlie, where are ya?! Charlie!

(Charlie hears his name, tenses, looks up.)

Young Charlie's Voice *(from Apartment above)*: I'm in the studio, writing.

Eddie: The studio. Is that the same as the toilet?

Young Charlie's Voice: Sometimes.

Eddie *(shouting)*: Charlie, *move* it, *now*, *pronto*, *down* here!

Young Charlie *(entering from Apartment)*: I'm coming, I'm in transit . . .

(Young Charlie, about eleven, concerned, thoughtful, and many worlds away, slouches down the stairs car-

rying a stack of loose-leaf pages and several pens; Eddie leans towards him confidentially.)

Eddie: Charlie, I got this problem; see, until your book comes out and you become a millionaire, I figured I'd still run my little business here . . . *(shouting)* so how about ya do the goddamn *set*-ups and help me *open* the place! The set-ups and the *mail*, Mister, you got obligations!

Young Charlie *(quietly getting tray of set-ups from bar)*: I got the mail already, it's by the register.

(Eddie exits, briskly, to work in Kitchen as Young Charlie begins to go rather distractedly about the task of placing set-ups on two or three tables; Charlie watches him silently, intently, for a few moments, then . . .)

Charlie: Jesus, they were right, I *didn't* pick up my feet. *(Leans towards him.)* The shuffling, what's with the *shuff*ling here? Straighten up, will ya? C'mon, Charlie, what happened to "No shit from nobody"?

Young Charlie *(a forlorn sigh, whispering)*: Oh-boy-oh-boy-oh-boy . . .

Charlie: I don't get it, in all the albums I'm always *smiling* . . . *(Nods thoughtfully.)* Yeah, but that's because they kept saying "smile" . . . *(Following, close to him, gently:)* Don't worry, kid, you're gettin' out. *Outa* here. Sooner than you think. What is it, money? You need money? Bucks, Charlie, *bucks*, the bucks are on their *way* . . . Oh, if I could just give you a coupla dollars, hand you a twenty, right now, a kinda loan, a . . . *(During the above, Young Charlie will have deposited several slugs in the Jukebox, punched the same key several times and crossed over to the "Vote Here for Miss Daitch, 1944" display where he is now clearly entranced, as always, by the face of Miss Daitch Contestant Number Two, Peggy Parsons, and the biography beneath it; we begin to hear the Helen Forrest–Dick Haymes recording of "Long Ago and Far Away" from the Jukebox, their voices drifting dreamily in the empty bar.)* Oh, my God . . . Peggy Parsons . . . *that's* it . . . *(Turns to us, as it all comes back.)* The Miss Daitch Contest of Forty-Four, our bar has been selected as one of the officially designated polling places in the neighborhood . . . *(Softly, from memory, as Young Charlie studies bio:)* "Pretty, perky, pert Peggy Parsons, or 'Peggo' as she prefers to be called, plans to pursue an acting career in motion pictures . . ." Peggo, Peggo . . . To say that I had a crush on Peggy Parsons would be to say that Mao Tse-Tung had a crush on Communism; only the beginning of July and I had already cast over six hundred ballots in the Greater New York area. *(Young Charlie sits in Charlie's usual booth, starts fervently re-writing whatever is on his loose-leaf pages, all of it clearly inspired by occasional glances at Peggy; the Music swells, filling the bar.)* Yeah, go with it, Charlie, this is it, it doesn't get better than this . . . *(Sits next to him in booth, leans close.)* Very important: love, Charlie, love does *not* make the world go round, *looking* for it does; this is important . . . Also very important, Charlie, in about ten years you're gonna meet a girl at the Museum of Modern Art, in front of the "Guernica"—let this painting be a *warning* to you—don't go out with this girl, don't even *talk* to this girl, by all means do *not marry this girl*—

Joey: Hey, Charlie—*(Hangs up phone, comes down towards booth.)* Been settin' up tickets for the guys, everybody tells me—

Young Charlie *(points to pages in Joey's pocket)*: Did you read it?

Joey: Charlie, *listen*, word's out, the Avengers, the Gladiators, they're gonna be roamin' tonight, like Memorial Day, or maybe like the Jew Hunt on Pell Street—whatever, I don't want you walkin' over to Rutgers Arena by yourself tonight. Gonna work out with Bimmy, then I come *back* for ya—are you listening?

Young Charlie: Yeah, after Bimmy's I go with you. Did you *read* it?

Joey: Sometimes, I tell ya, it's like you're not *present* here—

Young Charlie *(rising in booth)*: Did you read the *letter*, fa Chrissake!

Joey: I *read* the letter, I *read* the goddamn letter! It's completely nuts and wacko. Also hopeless and dumb.

Young Charlie: If you got a criticism, tell me.

Joey: Charlie, number one: I don't *get* it—*(Indicating the Miss Daitch photos.)* These girls, they all got the same *smile*, the same *eyes*, the same *nose*—*(Pointing.)* C'mon, tell me, what's the difference between Peggy Parsons . . . and "Lovely, lively Laurie Lipton" here?

Young Charlie: The difference? The *diff*erence? Why am I discussing this with a boxer?

Joey: I got to go to Bimmy's—

Young Charlie *(holds up loose-leaf pages)*: Thirty seconds, Joey—the revised version; I changed key words.

Joey *(leans against booth)*: Twenty.

Young Charlie *(reads from pages)*: "Mr. Samuel Goldwyn, Metro-Goldwyn-Mayer Studios. Dear Sam: Enclosed please find photo of Peggy Parsons. I think you will agree that this is the outstanding exquisiteness of a Motion Picture Star. You may reach her by the Daitch's Beer distribution place in your area is my belief. If Motion Picture employment is a result you may wish to say to her who recommended her eventually. She or yourself can reach me by post at the Flamingo Apartments, Six Eighty-One Canal Street, New York City. In closing I think of you first-hand instead of Darryl or David because of your nation of origin Poland which is right near my father's original nation Russia. Yours truly, C. E. Ross." *(Young Charlie does* *not look up from the letter, so concerned is he about his brother's response. Joey, sensing this, sits opposite him in the booth.)*

Joey: To begin with, that's an exceptionally well-put, well-written letter, Charlie . . .

Young Charlie: I know what you're thinkin', but *wild things* happen out there, Joey; they're findin' stars in *drug*stores, *ele*vators—

Joey: Right, and I'm sure the feeling you have for this Peggy is—

Young Charlie: Peggo, she prefers to be called Peggo—

Joey: Peggo, right—is genuine. So let's follow this through for a moment. Say, thousand-to-one shot, but Goldwyn, somebody in his office, sees the picture, say he gets a hold of her; say she's grateful, comes down here to Canal Street to see you, right?

Young Charlie: Right, right.

Joey: And you're eleven.

Young Charlie: Joey, I'm *aware* that there's an age problem; I will *deal* with it.

Joey *(after a moment, quietly)*: Tell ya, sometimes, the similarities, you and Pop, it scares the shit outa me, kid.

Young Charlie *(studying letter)*: Maybe "Dear Sam" 's too familiar; maybe "Dear Samuel" or "Mr. Goldwyn," huh?

Joey *(pats his shoulder)*: Right; that'll do it. *(Rises, starts briskly towards front door.)* Gotta get to Bimmy, I ain't worked out since the Chocolate Chopper. *(As Eddie enters, returning from work in Kitchen to go to stack of mail behind bar:)* See ya before the fight, Pop; comin' back to pick up Charlie.

Eddie *(looks up from mail)*: Hey, this kid tonight—an easy win, but the Bazooka's got a little weight on ya and I don't like his left—so go for the kill *early*; the *kill*, Joey. Remember, the boy is *nothin'*; he is *now*, he always *was*—

Joey *(as he exits into street)*:—and he always *will* be!

Charlie *(to us, from booth)*: Brother, brotherly, brotherhood: dynamite, powerhouse words, you could take them up off the ground like a punch; they meant—and still, now, at this moment, mean—Joey. However, take note, the only time Pop talks to me is when his prince is unavailable . . .

Eddie *(behind bar, studying a letter)*: Charlie, the *set*-ups, what happened? *(Young Charlie leaves booth to continue his task.)* You can stick the flags in the pineapples, O.K.? *(Young Charlie carries flags and tray of set-ups to center table; Eddie, still looking down at the letter, speaks quietly, solemnly.)* Charles . . .

(Young Charlie freezes at table.)

Charlie: "Charles," in this household, is my criminal name.

Eddie: Charles . . . I'm lookin' at a letter here from the Star of David School, Rabbi Rubin.

Young Charlie: These flags, Pop, they don't fit into the pineapples . . .

Eddie *(still looking down at letter, calmly)*: This is *some* letter, this letter. It's got my undivided attention.

Young Charlie: Hebrew's been over a week now, Pop; it don't start again till—

Eddie *(continuing calmly)*: Turns out it's been over for *you* a very long time now. About eight months, according to this letter. Also according to this letter there's been a lot of *other* letters. Says here, Rubin, "I had assumed from your past responses to my inquiries regarding Charles' religious training . . ." Turns out Rubin's been writin' to me, and I been *answerin'* him on this matter seven months now. Hey, I even got compliments on "the grace and wisdom of my remarks," says here. He *especially* likes the graciousness how I keep payin' him anyway even though you ain't goin' there no more.

Young Charlie: Pop, how about we—

Eddie *(still calmly, folding letter)*: Convenient for ya, you bein' the one gets the mail. Musta got distracted today, huh? Yeah. Bugsy Siegel don't get distracted, Frank Costello don't get distracted; Dillinger got distracted *once* . . . and now he's dead.

Young Charlie *(moving towards bar)*: Pop, I gotta tell ya—

Eddie: Charlie, look at my hands. Are ya lookin' at my hands?

Young Charlie: Yeah.

Eddie: What I'm doin' here is I'm holdin' onto the edge of the bar because if I let go I'm gonna beat the crap outa ya.

Young Charlie: Here's what—

Eddie: I'm here loadin' up shickers so you can hang out with God, twenty a month to the Star of David, hard cash, and you ain't even *there. (Quietly, in awe:)* While I'm *sayin'* it, I don't believe it. I don't believe that you're standin' there in front of me alive, I didn't kill you yet.

Young Charlie: It was *wrong*, the whole *thing*, I *know*, but lemme—

Eddie: My hands, they're lettin' go of the bar—*(Suddenly moving out from behind bar towards Young Charlie, Young Charlie backing up fearfully across the room, his hands raised, urgently.)*

Young Charlie: I gotta tell ya *one* thing, Pop, *one thing*!

Eddie *(after a moment)*: *One* thing.

Young Charlie *(keeping his distance; fervently)*: That place; you don't know what it *is* there, the Star of David. It's a terrible place. It's not even a Temple or anything. It's just this ratty place on Houston Street. This ratty room on the second floor of a building, two Rabbis in a room makin' a buck. Pop, I swear, God isn't there like you think.

Eddie: He's *there*, kid. Take my word for it—

Young Charlie: Over Pedro and Olga's *Dance* Studio? Two ratty guys with bad breath who throw chalk at your head and slam books on your hand every time you miss a trick? I mean real angry guys with bugs in their beards; sometimes they just kick you in the ass on general principles.

Eddie: Yeah, that's God all right; I'd know Him anywhere.

Young Charlie: That ain't God, those guys—

Eddie: Sure they ain't, I know that; but they're *connected*. That's the whole thing in life: *connections*, kid. *(Relaxes slightly, leans towards him.)* First thing, right off, I guarantee you, there's a God. You got that?

Young Charlie: I'm with you on that. We only disagree on where He's located.

Eddie: Hebrew School, He's located *there*; so you go back there. Sit. *(Young Charlie sits obediently at center table; Eddie sits opposite him.)* Because there's times —you're in trouble, you're really sick, and especially when you die, just before you die—you'll be glad you stayed in touch. That's the payoff. There's gonna be a time, guaranteed, you'll be grateful I made ya go, but the main thing is if ya don't go back I'm gonna kill ya.

Young Charlie: I don't get it, Pop. Ma lights the candles Friday, starts the prayer, ya say, "Cut the shit and let's eat"; ya *never* go to Temple anymore, the *bar* was open last Rosh Hashana, ya—

(Eddie suddenly grabs Young Charlie by the collar of his shirt with one hand and pulls him halfway across the table.)

Eddie: I stay in *touch*, Criminal! Look, you're makin' me grit my teeth! My goddamn *bridge* is crackin'! I stay in *touch*, Putzolla! Twenty a month to Rubin and the bandits so you should learn the worda the Torah and the worda God—

Young Charlie: I can't breathe, Pop—

Eddie: That's two shifts a month I'm puttin' out for God here exclusive, same like I done with Joey! Are you breathing?

Young Charlie: *No*—

Eddie: Then *breathe*—*(Lets him go.)* And I got married by a Rabbi, under God, twenty-five years and I stick! How *come* I stick? A woman, we all realize, is at this time a wacky person, nearly deaf; also a rough mouth don't encourage my endeavors whatever. *(Silence for a moment.)* This is currently. But there was occasions otherwise. *(Glances up at Apartment door, then leans towards Young Charlie; quietly:)* You hearda the expression "raven-haired"? O.K., there's some girls got hair they call "midnight black," very beautiful, but it got no light in it, see. "Raven-hair" is like the bird, glossy, light come *out* of it, got its own light comin' out—this is what she had. First time I seen her she's runnin' down these steps to the beach, this hair is down to her ass, flyin' behind her like wings, her arms is out like she's gonna hug the entire Black Sea, laughin' . . . *(Slaps the table.)* And then, Sonny-Boy, minutes, *minutes*—I swear to you, minutes after the Rabbi pronounced us the lights went out in her hair like somebody turned off a switch; and the mouth began. Continuing in this manner until she became the totally wacky deaf person we know in our home at this time; she is at this *moment* upstairs, stirring a pot, getting wackier and deafer. But I *stick*! *(Slaps the table again.)* That's my point, kid: I *stick*. Because there'll be a night one day when the heart attack comes and somebody'll have to call Dr. Schwartzman and the ambulance. And who will do it? The Wacky Ravenhead! In five minutes she covers a fifty-year bet! Why? Because I put my money on a good woman. Wacky and deaf; but good. There's a lot of people got this kind of arrangement. It's called a Coronary Marriage. And when you find a better reason for people staying together, let me know. Love; forget it. Who are they kidding? It won't be there when you get home and it won't call Dr. Schwartzman for you. *(Leans closer.)* Same with God. I *stick*. *I* stick and so will you. Because all God's gotta do is come through *once* to make Him worth your time. Maybe twice. Just one big deal and once when you die so you ain't scared shitless. *(Picks up letter.)* O.K., you hang in with Rubin till the Bar Mitzvah shot. Whatta we talkin' about?—a coupla years, tops, it's *over*; you're joined up with *my* Pop and *his* Pop and *his* and all the Pops back forever—you're covered, it's set, I done my job; then ya do whatever the hell ya want. *(Holds out his hand.)* Deal? *(A moment, then Young Charlie shakes his hand; Eddie rises, starts briskly back towards bar.)* C'mon, let's seal it. *(Young Charlie follows him, Eddie goes behind bar.)* Mine's vodka. What'll ya have?

Young Charlie *(sits opposite him, elbows on bar)*: Let's see . . . you got lemon juice and seltzer?

Eddie: Like the choice; *I* got it—*(A spritz, a splash, places it on bar.)* Now *you* got it. *(Pouring his vodka.)* Yeah, good; I think this was a good conversation.

Young Charlie: Me too . . . I mean it ain't exactly Andy Hardy and the Judge, but it's somethin'. *(He laughs at his own joke; soon Eddie laughs too, joining him, they "click" glasses.)* Boy, Pop, you're right—

Eddie *(still laughing)*: *Sure* I'm right—

Young Charlie *(still laughing)*: I mean about Mom, she sure is *some* wacky *deaf* person; I mean, she—

(A sudden, resounding smack in the face from Eddie sends Young Charlie reeling off his bar-stool, knocking him to the floor. Charlie, in his booth, holds his cheek, feeling the impact.)

Eddie *(shouting)*: You will not mock your mother! Even in jest!

Young Charlie *(half-mumbling, still on his knees, his head still ringing, shocked and hurt at once)*: Hell with you, *hell* with you, don't make no sense . . .

Eddie *(comes out from behind bar, thundering, pointing down at him)*: What's *that*? What do I hear?! Gypsies! Gypsies! The Gypsies brought ya! This can't be mine!

Young Charlie *(scrambling to his feet, screaming)*: Oh, I wish to God they *had*! I wish to God the Gypsies brought me! I don't wanna be from *you*! *(Darting from table to table as Eddie stalks him, the boy gradually rising to full, wailing, arm-flailing rage.) Nothin'* fits together, nothin' ya *say*! Goddamn switch*er*oo alla time! *Her? Her? You! You're* the crazy one, *you're* the deaf one, *you're* the one nobody can talk to! *(Whacking pineapples off of tables, wildly, screaming, pointing fiercely at Eddie.)* Loser! Loser! Goddamn *loser*! You're a goddamn crazy *loser* in a goddamn loser *shit*house here!

(Eddie suddenly snaps, a moment of pure madness, races towards him, grabbing a chair, raising it over his head, clearly about to smash it down on Young Charlie; Young Charlie drops to the ground, his arms over his head, Eddie lost in rage, all his enemies below him.)

Eddie *(roaring): You people . . . !*

(Eddie freezes, about to strike, looks down, sees that it's Young Charlie; he slowly lowers the chair, trembling with rage, looking at it, realizing for a moment what he was about to do, shaken, quite still; he tosses the chair to the ground.)

Young Charlie *(rises, unaware of what's happening to his father)*: Come on, great, let's see ya do the one thing ya *can* do . . . *(Shouting, his fists raised, holding his ground.)* No. No more hitting this year. This is *it* . . . Come on, come on, Pop . . . just one more move, I'm the perfect height; just one more move and I kick you in the balls so hard ya don't straighten up for a *month* . . . *(Full power now.)* One more move and it's right in the balls—right in the *balls*, Pop, I swear to God!

Eddie: Swear to who?!

Young Charlie: God! I swear to God!

Eddie *(after a moment, quietly)*: See how He comes in handy? *(A pause; then, still a bit shaken, covering.)* Well, I . . . I believe I've made my point. Sometimes ya gotta illustrate, y'know . . . for the full clarity of the thing. *(Sound of Gusta approaching from the Apartment above, humming a few phrases of "In Odessa," Eddie heading briskly back to bar, pulling himself together.)* Now you'll excuse me, I gotta open in five minutes. First day of the Flamingo Lounge.

(Eddie takes a quick shot of the vodka he left on the bar, erasing the episode, returning to work as Gusta enters from the Apartment carrying her usual two large pots of just-cooked food, humming brightly, Young Charlie eventually retreating slowly, thoughtfully, to his booth and his loose-leaf pages.)

Gusta *(placing pots on Kitchen stove)*: Today we got the usuals, Eddie—Mulligan Stew, Cottage Fries, General Patton's Pancakes, D-Day Dumplings—

Eddie: General Patton's Pancakes, I forget—

Gusta: Potato Latkes—

Eddie: Potato Latkes, right—

Gusta *(bringing plate of food to Young Charlie's booth)*: Upstairs, simmering, I got for Joey's party tonight— it's just us, Eddie, I'll use maiden names—Kasha-Varnishkes, also Holishkes with honey and raisin.

Eddie: Great, Gloria, great—

Gusta *(starts back towards Kitchen)*: Joey's boxing-fight, I'll be upstairs; you'll inform me at knockout time, I bring down the food.

Eddie: Don't worry, this guy won't *touch* him, Gloria—

Gusta: This is how it is with me: I can't watch, so I can't listen either; it hurts.

Eddie *(approaching her at Kitchen doorway; quietly)*: Hey, for the party tonight, how about ya take the pins outa y'hair . . . let it, y'know, free.

Gusta: I let it free it goes in the soup.

Eddie: I mean, just loose, y'know, like flowin'.

Gusta: Who's gonna *see*, Finney, Nick—?

Eddie: *Me, I'll* see it—

Gusta *(suddenly)*: Eddie, there's a bird on the ceiling.

Eddie: It's a *flamingo*.

Gusta: All right, I'll believe you; it's a flamingo. Why is it on the ceiling?

Eddie: Gonna be like a *symbol* for us, Gloria, for the place; like I was tellin' Joey: Borden's got a cow, Billingsley's got a stork, Firestone—

Gusta: How much did the dopey bird cost?

Eddie: It just so happens this hand-made, hand-crafted, sixty-eight-light Flamingo Chandelier is the only one of its kind in the world.

Gusta: Two is hard to imagine. *(She goes to Kitchen stove; Eddie continues, high with "Opening Day" fever.)*

Eddie: Gloria, I'm talkin' to Joey this mornin', somethin' *come* to me—somethin' for the *place*, somethin' we never *tried* before—a *word*, *one* word, a magic word's gonna make all the difference!

Gusta: Fire.

Eddie: Advertising!

Gusta: We'll burn it down and get the insurance. The Moose *alone* puts us in clover. *(Exits deep into Kitchen, out of sight.)*

Eddie: *Advertising!* Advertising, kiddo! *(Exits into Kitchen, pursuing her, inspired; we hear his voice from inside, his enthusiasm building.)* I'm talkin' about a small ad, classy, in there with the Clubs, Gloria—just a picture of a flamingo, *one* word: *"Lounge,"* under it; under *that* "Six Eighty-One Canal"—like everybody *knows* already, like it's *in*, Gloria—

Charlie *(during above, rising from booth, moving towards Kitchen)*: Leave her alone, Pop, leave her *alone*, it's never gonna *happen*—

Eddie's Voice: Guy comes in here regular, works for the "Journal-American," runs a heavy tab, I trade him on the *space*, kid—

Charlie *(during above, louder and louder)*:—stop, we're never going Uptown; stop, *stop* driving us *crazy* with it, Eddie—this *bar*, this goddamn *bar!*

Young Charlie *(at booth, writing, as Eddie's voice continues)*: "Dear Mr. Zanuck . . . it would not be perfectly candid of me if I did not frankly admit and advise you that I have just previously contacted Sam on this exact matter . . ."

Charlie *(turns, anguished, caught between the two of them)*: My God, you're just as crazy as *he* is . . .

Young Charlie *(writing, his confidence building)*: ". . . I refer to the enclosed Peggy Parsons. We live in a competitive industry, Darryl, and I do not wish to keep this woman in a basket . . ."

(We begin to hear the sound of about Twenty Teen-aged Boys' Voices, quite distantly at first, far down the street outside, singing happily, with great gusto; the sound of the Voices and their song growing louder and louder, reaching a peak as we hear them pass the front door, then fading out as they continue along Canal Street; Young Charlie completely oblivious to this sound as he continues to write his letter, Charlie gradually caught by the sound of the Boys' Voices, the song drawing him slowly down to the front door as the passing Voices reach their peak; all lights dimming far down now except for the remaining full light on Charlie at the front door, his face mirroring his almost forgotten but now vividly remembered helplessness and fear at the sound of the Boys' Voices and their song.)

Twenty Boys' Voices *(to the tune of the Marine Corps Hymn)*:
"On the shores of Coney Island
While the guns of freedom roar,
The Sheenies eat their Matzo Balls
And make money off the war,
While we Christian saps go fight the Japs,
In the uniforms they've made.
And they'll sell us Kosher hot dogs
For our victory parade.
So it's onward into battle
They will send us Christian slobs,

When the war is done and victory won,
All the Jews will have our jobs."

(Sound of laughter, a crash of glass, then cheering as the Boys' Voices fade into the night.)

Charlie *(shouts towards the fading Voices)*: If Joey was here . . . if Joey was here you'd never get away with it!

(The Boys' Voices are quickly obliterated by the sudden sound of a Cheering Crowd, raucous and enthusiastic, and the machine-gun voice of Ringside sportscaster Speed Spector blasting out the blow-by-blow of a fight in progress, the tiny yellow light of the Philco radio dial popping on in the darkness and then glowing brighter as the Cheering Crowd, Spector's Voice and all the bar-lights come up full to reveal that night's Party and the Party Guests: Hannah, Nick and Finney, gathered about the radio, Eddie entering from the Kitchen holding two champagne bottles aloft on a tray full of fancy glasses, a silk vest added to his usual Uptown Bartender's white shirt and black bow-tie, Zaretsky entering somewhat later from the Apartment above wearing an old but splendid smoking-jacket and cravat for the occasion; Charlie remaining at front door looking off towards street, Young Charlie no longer onstage.)

Spector's Voice *(from Philco, breathless, one long sentence)*: . . . toe to toe and here they *go* fourth round another *fight* friends *first* three bouts waltz-time dancin' *darlings* number *four* we got a slammin' *slug*

fest here Killer Kalish and Homicide Hennesy tradin'
solid *body* shots insteada *party* favors here tonight
forty-five seconds into frame *four* . . . (*Charlie being
gradually pulled away from the front door by the much
pleasanter memory of Spector's Voice*) . . . carryin' it to
Kalish lightnin' *left* rockin' *right* a stick a stick a jab a
hook hook hook roundhouse *right* Killer's outa *business* . . .

Charlie (*to us, as Spector and Cheering Crowd continue*): Well, they didn't call him Speed Spector for
nothin', did they? And tonight we waited for *that voice*
to talk about *my* brother. First, however, would be the
usual pre–Main Event interview with Big Mike Baskin
of Big Mike Baskin's Broadway Boys' and Men's
Clothes, sponsor of the Tuesday Night Amateurs. We,
of course, all knew him as the former Manny Buffalino
of Buffalino's Grand Street Garments who gave a
silver-plated watch to each of the winners . . . and a
terrible headache to Pop.

Spector's Voice: . . . whatta ya think about that
whoppin' big *win*, Big Mike?

Big Mike's Voice: Spid, dis boy, alla tonight win'
gonna get a sil'-plate wash froma Big Mike. Now, he
don' like dis wash, he can hocka dis wash for fifteen
doll'—

Eddie (*entering with champagne*): Can't stand the
mouth on that greaseball—(*Turns radio volume way
down; they all protest.*) Don't worry, Joey's bout ain't

on for five minutes anyways—goddamn Steerage *Green*horn; twenty-six locations, man's sittin' on a coupla mil—*nobody* knows what the hell he's *talkin'* about! What's his *angle*, how's he *do* it—?

Finney *(as Zaretsky enters, slapping Zaretsky on back)*: Evenin', Mr. Z.; how's Show Business?

Zaretsky: Mr. Finney; Abbott and *Costello* are in Show Business, Amos and even *Andy* are in Show Business, Franklin Delano *Roose*velt is in Show Business—

Finney *(pinching Zaretsky's cheek)*: Lost me bearin's, darlin', it's the joy of the night—

Eddie *(placing bottles on center table)*: I say sixty seconds into Round One this champagne is pourin' and Gloria's down with the goodies!

Hannah: And Nick wears the *shirt* tonight.

Eddie: Great . . .

Finney: The shirt, of course . . .

Hannah: The occasion demanded.

Zaretsky: This then is a shirt of some significance, I assume.

Nick: Oh, ya might say. Ya might well say, Mr. Za-retsky. (*Opening old jacket to reveal a faded yellow shirt instead of his usual faded white shirt; there are dark brown stains on the shoulder and collar.*) For this then is the blood of Barney Ross, spilled the night he lost the World Welterweight to Armstrong, the greatest Losin' Win I ever saw.

Eddie: Greatest Losin' Win in the history of the fight game.

Finney: Easy.

Nick: Second *row* we are, the four of us; May Thirty-One, Nineteen Thirty-Eight, Round Five, his legs said goodbye to the man, never to return in what was t'be the last bout o' Barney's life. Ref Donovan's beggin' Ross to let 'im stop the thing—"No," Barney says, through the blood in his mouth, "I'm the Champ, he'll have to beat me in the *ring* and *not* on a stool in m'corner!" There then come ten rounds of a horror ya never want to see again, but proud ya saw the once for the grandness that was in it, the crowd is quiet and many look away, but at the end the cheers is for Barney who lost his title and won his pride. (*Looking about at his friends.*) Which is why we call it, the four of us . . .

Nick, Eddie, Finney: . . . the Greatest Losin' Win we ever saw!

Hannah: In my case, heard.

Finney: It was in the Twelfth Barney's blood hit the shirt—

Hannah: A thundering right from Armstrong, yes—

Eddie: Ya *get* it, Actor—ya see why me and my boys are called *Ross* now?

Finney *(suddenly turns to radio)*: My God, the *fight*—

Eddie: Oh, *shit*—*(He dashes to the radio, quickly turns up volume.)*

(We hear the sound of the Cheering Crowd as Eddie turns the volume up full, the sound building louder and louder as the Crowd chants rhythmically; Charlie sits solemnly in his booth, nodding, remembering it all too well.)

The Crowd: Chicken *Pete* . . . Chicken *Pete* . . . Chicken *Pete* . . .

Hannah *(confused, frightened)*: Chicken Pete, Nick? . . .

Spector's Voice *(shouting above the chanting Crowd)*: . . . Listen to *that*, Fans! *New* one on Old *Speed* here; got a Referee, one fighter, whole crowd, packed Arena—*one* thing missing: the *other fighter*! Pistol Pete is *not* in that ring, *not* in the locker room, *no*where to be found, friends . . .

(All in bar-room stunned at first; Eddie, the others, not moving, riveted by the information as it comes out of the radio; the sound of the chanting Crowd building, filling the room.)

Spector's Voice: . . . Ref Gordon tells me Pistol Pete's not in the *building*, no *message*, no *word; sounds* like the best explanation of this one's comin' from the crowd itself . . .

The Crowd *(louder and louder)*: . . . Chicken *Pete* . . . Chicken *Pete* . . . Chicken *Pete* . . .

Finney *(bewildered, staring into radio)*: He didn't *show*, Joey didn't *show* . . .

(The sound of stomping and clapping joins the rhythmic chant of the Crowd now as Eddie moves slowly out from behind the bar, carefully controlling his fear and confusion.)

Eddie *(quietly, evenly)*: He's hurt, he's hurt . . . out *cold*; he'd have to be out *cold* to stay away from that bout . . . he's hurt . . . *(Moving towards phone.)* *Bimmy's*, maybe somebody at Bimmy's, somebody knows . . .

Zaretsky: He leaves with Chaim for the Arena, this is an hour ago . . .

Finney: I heard them Avenger boys was gatherin' on Pell . . .

Hannah: Nit do gedacht . . .

Nick *(rising from stool)*: I go to the Precinct, get some of the fellahs . . .

Eddie *(picking up phone)*: Yeah, yeah . . .

The Crowd *(building to peak now)*: . . . Chicken *Pete* . . . Chicken *Pete* . . . Chicken *Pete* . . .

(The front door bursts open and Joey rushes in, followed by Young Charlie; though somewhat shaken, there is something decisive, resolved in Joey as he stands tensely at the center of the room, his "Pistol Pete" jacket gripped in his hand; Young Charlie, clearly bewildered by the evening's events, stays close to his brother.)

Hannah *(trembling)*: Jussel, Jussel . . . ?

Joey *(gently)*: Everything's fine, Hannah.

Eddie *(starts towards him; quietly)*: Thank God, you're O.K. . . . you're O.K. . . .

Joey: I'm not O.K. *(Races behind the bar towards the sound of the chanting Crowd, snaps off the radio; the room is silent.)* I will be.

Eddie: The *fight*, kid, the *fight* . . . what the hell *happened* . . . ?

Joey (*slaps his jacket onto the bar, grabs up vodka bottle and shot-glass*): No more fights. No more fights, Pop. Not here. (*Fills his shot-glass, downs it.*)

Eddie: Not *here*? Not *here*? What the hell does *that* mean? I need some *explainin'* here, kid, I gotta—

Zaretsky: Let him *speak*, Itzik.

Joey (*quietly*): Pop, this mornin', workin' out with Bimmy—

Eddie: To*night*, kid, I wanna know about to*night*—

Joey (*continuing, firmly*): This mornin', workin' out with Bimmy, we're skippin', we're sparrin', my mind ain't there, Pop. I'm doin' math. Three hundred and fifty thousand Jews in twenty-one days, comes out seventeen thousand five hundred a day, *this* day, today—

Eddie: A buncha crazy *stories*, Joey, I told ya—(*Wheeling on Zaretsky.*) *You*, it's you and your goddamn *bull*shit—

Joey (*moving towards him*): Please, ya gotta be quiet, Pop. That's maybe two thousand just while I'm workin' out. Seventeen thousand five hundred a day. No, it's impossible, I figure; Pop's *right*, it's nuts. I keep punchin' the bag. I come back to pick up Charlie, we're headin' over, not Seven yet; then I hear people hollerin', I look up, I see it. Top of the "Forward" Buildin',

tallest damn buildin' around here, there's the "Jewish
Daily Forward" sign, y'know, big, maybe thirty feet
high and wide as the buildin', electric bulbs, ya can see
it even deep into Brooklyn, *forever*, Pop. What they did
is they took out the right bulbs, exactly the right bulbs,
gotta be hundreds of 'em, so instead of "Jewish Daily
Forward" the sign says: "Jew Is For War"; it's goddamn blazin' over the city, Pop, and Charlie and me
start runnin' towards it, we're still maybe eight blocks
away, we're passin' alotta people and kids on Canal,
pointin' up, laughin', some cheerin', "Son of a *bitch*, son
of a *bitch*, we fight the *war* and the Jews get *rich*," a
guy grabs my arm, smilin', musta seen me box, guy my
age, he says, "Pete, Pete, let's go get us some Yids,
Pete!" and I know that second for sure they are doin'
seventeen thousand five hundred a day, somewhere,
seventeen thousand five hundred a day and I'm a guy
spends his time boppin' kids for a silver-plated watch
from Big Mike, hockable for fifteen dollars; right now
I wouldn't hock me for a dime. Point is, I'm goin' in,
Pop. I'm gettin' into this war and I need your help,
now. *(Eddie is silent.)* Army don't register me till next
month, then it could be a year, more, before they call
me. *Navy*, Pop, Navy's the game; they take ya at seventeen with a parent's consent. Eight A.M. tomorrow
I'm at Ninety Church, I pick up the consent form, you
fill it out, sign it, ten days later Boot Camp at Lake
Geneva, September I'm in it, Pop. Korvette, Destroyer,
Sub-chaser, whatever, *in* the goddamn thing.

Eddie *(after a moment)*: Your mother will never—

Joey: I just need you, Pop. One parent. One signature. *(Silence for a moment.)* Do me a favor; take a look outside. Just turn left and look at the sky.

(During Joey's story, Hannah has moved instinctively closer to Nick, holding his arm; Zaretsky rises.)

Zaretsky: Come then, Itzik.

(Eddie turns towards the door; Zaretsky crosses to the door, exits into street, followed after a moment by Eddie and then Finney; Nick starts to go but Hannah whispers fearfully to him.)

Hannah: Stay with me, Nick. They'll look, they'll describe.

Nick *(embracing her)*: Sure, darlin', sure . . .

(Silence for a few moments; Charlie, in his booth, watching the two boys.)

Young Charlie: You didn't tell me that part . . . about goin' in. You didn't mention that.

Joey: It come to me, Charlie.

Young Charlie *(urgently)*: Lotta guys to fight *here*, y'know, the Avengers, the Gladiators; ya don't have to go all the way to *Europe*, ya—

(Eddie enters, crosses slowly to bar, sits on stool; he is followed by Finney, and then Zaretsky who remains at doorway looking out into street.)

Finney *(to Hannah and Nick)*: Hangin' over town like a second bloody moon, it is.

Eddie *(after a moment, slapping bar)*: Get me the goddamn paper, I sign it *now*. Go down to Ninety Church Street, wake the Putzes *up*, bring me the form and I sign it now. All I ask, kid, you're over there, you kill a couple for your Pop, *personally*. *(Starts towards Joey; fiercely:)* Kill 'em, Joey, *kill* 'em. *Show* 'em, kid, show 'em how a Jew fights.

Joey *(grabs Eddie's fist, holds it proudly in the air)*: And in this corner, wearin' the green trunks—The East Side Savage!

(All cheering, patting Joey on the back, except for Zaretsky and the two Charlies.)

Young Charlie *(looking anxiously from one to the other)*: Everybody goin' so *fast* here, so *fast*—

Nick: Try to get home for Christmas, kid—

Young Charlie: They got *reasons*, y'know, why they don't take guys till they're eighteen, they got—

Joey *(turns to Zaretsky, who has remained silent at front door)*: You're *with* me, aren't ya?

Zaretsky *(after a moment)*: Yes . . . *yes*, were I your age—*(Joey rushes forward, embraces him.)*

Eddie *(holding champagne bottle aloft, rallying the Group)*: Hey, hey, *hey*—we still got a *party* goin' here —a *better* one—goddamn Warrior's *send*-off we got here! *(Pops cork at center table as all gather round, except for Young Charlie who moves slowly over to his usual booth, sits near Charlie.)* First-class Frog juice we got here—*I* got it—*(Pouring for Joey first.)* Now *you* got it, kid—*(As he pours for the others:)* Hey, this ain't just Bazooka Kil*bane* goin' down—I'm talkin' about the whole goddamn Nazi-Nip *War* Machine here! *(Raising his glass.)* To the Winnah and still Cham*peen*!

Hannah *(raising her glass)*: So what's wrong with the Bounding Main?

Nick *(raising his glass)*: Right! To the Navy!

Finney *(raising his glass)*: To the Navy and Victory!

All *(loudly, raising glasses)*: The Navy and Victory!

(They click glasses just as Gusta enters from the Apartment above carrying a large tray of Party-food; starts down stairs, confused, seeing Joey amongst the Group.)

Gusta: The boxing-fight, Joey, you won already? Nobody informed me. *(They all turn to her, their six glasses held aloft, poised; she stops near Joey.)* Ah, no marks; good. O.K., Party-treats—*(Goes briskly to down left table, a distance from the Group, starts taking dishes from tray, placing them on table, her back to them; they all remain quite still, watching her.)* First, of course, basics: we got Kasha-Varnishkes, we got Holishkes, special for Mr. Zaretsky we got Kartoffel Chremsel with a touch apple . . .

Hannah *(quietly)*: Eddie signs a paper, Gusta, Joey goes to war.

Gusta *(a pause; then she continues briskly)*: We got Lokshen Kugel, we got a little Brisket Tzimmes with honey, special for Charlie we got Cheese Blintzes, a side sour cream . . .

Joey *(softly, moving towards her)*: Ma, did you hear that, Ma . . . ?

Gusta: And special for Finney and Nick—why not, I was in the mood—we got Mamaligele Rumanye with a smash strawberry.

Joey: Ma . . .

Gusta *(a moment; she turns to him)*: I hear everything, Sonny. You got some good news for me? *(Looks over at the Group.)* I hear it all. It's just that twenty years ago I started making selections. *(Walking slowly towards the Group.)* You see, if I listened, I would want to speak. And who would hear me? Who would hear me? Who would *hear* me?

(She slaps Eddie hard across the face. A beat; we hear the sudden sound of a full Marching Band and a Male Chorus doing a blasting, drum-rolling, lusty-voiced rendition of "Anchors Aweigh" as all lights fade quickly down on the frozen Party Group and the still figures of Gusta and Eddie, Music continuing at full volume.)

Male Chorus:

"Anchors aweigh, my boys,
Anchors aweigh,
Farewell to college joys,
We sail at break of day, day, day, day . . ."

(During Charlie's next speech the pulsing Jukebox lights will come up again and with them the half-light in which we will see only Eddie and Young Charlie remaining onstage and making those changes in the bar-room that would have occurred during the thirteen months till the next scene begins: Eddie solemnly draping a length of black ribbon about the frame of the grinning F.D.R. photo, then proudly hanging a map of the Pacific Theatre of War over the Jukebox, happily placing several blue and white Service Stars about the room, including one over Joey's boxing photo, finally exiting into Kitchen; Young Charlie will take down the Miss Daitch Display—being careful to keep the Peggy Parsons photo which he stores, among other treasures, in the hollow seat of the booth he and Charlie usually use. Charlie will have moved down towards us only a moment after the blackout on the Party Scene, humming a few phrases of "Anchors Aweigh" along with the

Jukebox, then speaking immediately to us during the action described above.)

Charlie: Joey called the shot exactly: September, he was in it—desperately trying to promote his way onto a Convoy-Korvette in the European Theatre, he ended up on a Destroyer in the Pacific and, as Joey pointed out, the only dangerous German he ever got to face was our dentist, Dr. Plaut—but he was *in* it; and, finishing ten weeks of Gunnery School in four, he became quickly known aboard the Destroyer Campbell as "The King Of The Twin-Forties"—double-mounted antiaircraft machine-guns in a swiveling steel bucket operated by a Gunner and an Ammo Man—*(Here replicated by Young Charlie holding two broom handles atop a spinning bar-stool.)* Yes, Joey was proud and brave and good and strong—but mostly, he was *gone*. *(Young Charlie puts on the "Pistol Pete" jacket Joey left on the bar, his posture noticeably straightening.)* He was gone and *I* was here, the house was mine. I was *it*: star of the show, Top of the Card, the Main Event. Civilians look for job openings in wartime . . . and there was an opening here for Prince.

(Charlie turns to center as lights come up on Young Charlie alone onstage, seated comfortably on bar-stool, his feet up, legs crossed at the ankle, on bar, gazing critically at the huge painting of the Four Poker Players over the bar-mirror. Sound of Harry Truman's Voice fading up with the lights as "Anchors Aweigh" record ends on Jukebox.)

Truman's Voice: . . . on Hiroshima, a military base. We won the race of discovery against the Germans. We have used it in order to shorten the agony of war, in order to save the lives of thousands and thousands of young Americans. We shall *continue* to use it until we completely destroy Japan's power to make war . . .

Eddie *(bursts in from Kitchen)*: The Atomic Cocktail, Charlie! *(Holds aloft two large containers of freshly mixed cocktails.) Two* kindsa rum, light *and* dark, shot o' grenadine—pineapple juice and coconut cream, give a kinda Tropical-Pacific feel. *(Sets containers and handmade placard on bar.)* Whatta ya think, kid?

Young Charlie *(still looking at Poker Picture, thoughtfully)*: That's a terrible painting, Pop.

Eddie *(reads from placard—he's illustrated it with a classic mushroom-cloud Hiroshima photo from a newspaper)*: "Atomic Cocktail—One Dollar—If the First Blast Don't Get You, the Fallout Will." How about that, Charlie?

Young Charlie *(squints at Poker Picture)*: Not only poorly painted, but look at all the *room* it takes up.

Eddie: What?

Young Charlie: This painting here, Pop; it's no good.

Eddie: What're ya talkin' about? This here's a hand-painted oil picture, seven feet by *six*, fits *exact* over the mirror. This is an original by goddamn Lazlo *Shim*kin; run up a big tab, gimme the picture on a trade-off. Got any idea what this thing's *worth* today?

Young Charlie: Nothin', Pop.

Eddie: Listen, Putz, this picture been sittin' up there since a year before you was *born*. You seen it every day o' ya *life*—all of a sudden it's no *good*?

Young Charlie: Yes; strange, isn't it?

Eddie *(quietly)*: I gotta open the bar in twenty minutes; otherwise I would immediately take the picture out in the alley and burn it. Only thing I can suggest to you in the meantime, Charlie, is that you *spend the rest of your goddamn life lookin' the other way!* *(Leaning towards him.)* Gypsies! Gypsies! The *Gypsies* left ya at my *door*step! *This* can't be *mine*! Before this personally autographed Lazlo *Shim*kin picture goes, *you* go. *(Points.)* *Feet* off the bar, and finish the set-ups.

Zaretsky *(entering from Apartment above)*: Ah, I sense artistic differences in the air.

Young Charlie *(starts working on set-ups)*: 'Morning, Mr. Zaretsky.

Zaretsky: Chaim, you have not yet, I trust, fetched the mail? *(Young Charlie shakes his head.)* Good then, it shall be my task. I expect today a cable from Buenos

Aires, in Argentina, where still exist two hundred thousand speakers of Yiddish, there confirming my appearance, a full three weeks of concerts; my first since the War. *(Starts towards front door.)*

Young Charlie *(impressed as always)*: Hey, Argen*tina* . . . Great.

Eddie *(stacking glasses)*: Three weeks without ya, Anton; breaks my goddamn heart. Don't worry, babe, we'll keep y'room *just* the way ya left it.

Zaretsky: Unfortunately. *(Opens front door.)* A room in which, for twelve years, sunlight has appeared almost entirely by metaphor. *(Exits into street. Silence for a moment.)*

Eddie *(his back to Young Charlie, busily stacking glasses)*: O.K., just for laughs, Putz, what's so ugly about that picture?

Young Charlie: For one thing, the light, Pop . . . *(Eddie squints at the painting.)* It's all like . . . flat, see. It's like the light is coming from *every*where, y'know, so it's not really—

Eddie: Yeah, right, O.K., good this come up. This stuff about where the light's comin' from, also these here poems and stories you been writin'. Take a for-instance—*(takes folded piece of loose-leaf paper from cash-register)* this poem ya give me Father's Day.

Young Charlie: Did ya like it? Ya never mentioned—

Eddie: Sure, sure. *(Hands it to him, sits at their usual center table.)* Do y'Pop a favor, O.K.? You read this to me, then I'm gonna ask ya a question. *(Young Charlie hesitates for a moment.)* Go ahead.

(Young Charlie starts to read as Zaretsky returns with the mail, places all but a few pieces on bar, listens attentively to poem.)

Young Charlie *(reading)*: O.K. . . . "Father of the Flamingo; by C. E. Ross: . . . He leadeth them beside distilled waters, he restoreth their credit; and if they be Mick Shickers, he maketh them to lie down in dark gutters. And yea, though I may walk through the valley of the shadow of Little Italy, I shall fear no Goy or evil sound, 'cause my Pop has taught me how to bring one up from the ground."

Zaretsky *(applauding)*: Bravo, Chaim; bravo! *(He exits upstairs, continuing to nod his approval for the work of a fellow artist.)*

Eddie: O.K., very nice. *(Leaning forward, pleasantly:)* O.K., now all I'm askin' is a truthful answer: who helped ya out with that?

Young Charlie: Nobody, Pop. I mean, it's a Twenty-Third Psalm take-off, so I got help from the *Bible*—

Eddie: I *know* that, *besides* that—the thing, the *ideas* in there, how it come together there—you tellin' me nobody helped ya out on that, the *Actor, no*body?

Young Charlie: Nobody, Pop.

Eddie *(he pauses, then indicates the chair opposite him; Young Charlie sits)*: O.K., there's times certain Jewish words is unavoidable, I give ya two: Narrishkeit and Luftmensh. Narrishkeit is stuff be*yond* foolish—like what?—your mother givin' English lessons, this would be Narrish-work. Now this Narrishkeit is generally put out by Luftmensh—meanin', literal, *guys* who live on the *air*—from which we get the term "no visible goddamn means of support." Poem-writers, story-writers, picture-painters, we got *alotta* 'em come in here; what ya got is mainly y'Fairies, y'Bust-Outs and y'Souseniks—a blue *moon*, ya get a sober straight-shooter, breaks even. *(Slaps the table.)* Now, I'm lookin' at this poem two months now, besides takin' note, numerous situations, how you *present* y'self, kid —first-class, flat-out *amazin'*, this poem. *(Young Charlie smiles happily, Eddie taps his son's head.)* It's goddamn Niagara *Falls* in there—now all we gotta do is point it the right way so ya can turn on a coupla *light* bulbs with it. The *answer*? Head like yours, ya know it already, don't ya?

Young Charlie *(confused but flattered)*: No; I don't, Pop.

Eddie: I speak, of course, of the Legal Profession! Brain like that, how you get them words together, I'm talkin' *Up*town, Charlie, I'm talkin' about the firm o' Ross, Ross, Somebody and *Some*body; you're gonna be walkin' through places the dollars stick to your *shoes*, y'can't *kick* the bucks off. Hey, looka the experience you got already, huh?—*(rises, arms wide, delightedly struck by the perfect illustration)*—twelve years now you been pleadin' cases before the bar!

(Eddie laughs happily at his joke, slapping the bar, Young Charlie laughing with him, their laughter building with the sharing of the joke, Charlie joining them.)

Charlie *(chuckling)*: Not bad, not bad; one for *you*, Pop . . . *(Suddenly frightened, remembering; he shouts:)* Now—it was *now*—

(We hear Gusta scream from upstairs—a long, wrenching, mournful wail, like the siren of a passing ambulance—even at this distance, a stairway and a closed door between them, the sound permeates the bar-room. Then silence; Eddie and Young Charlie frozen for a moment, then both racing towards the bottom of the stairs. Before they can reach the first step, though, Zaretsky enters at the top of the stairs from the Apartment above, closing the door quietly behind himself. Eddie and Young Charlie remain quite still, several feet from the stairs; Zaretsky takes a step or two down towards them.)

Zaretsky: The telegram I opened was not for me, Itzik. It is for you and Gusta. Jussel is dead. He was killed two days ago. The first telegram says only *(he reads)*: "The Secretary of War desires me to express his deep regret that your son, Petty Officer Second-Class Joseph Ross, was killed in action in defense of his country on August Sixth, Nineteen Forty-Five." *(A moment.)* Gusta stays upstairs; she requests to be alone for a while. *(Eddie and Young Charlie remain standing quite still at the bottom of the stairs, their backs to us, not a tremor, their emotions unreadable.)* There is more; shall I go on? *(Eddie nods.)* Enclosed also, a cable, this from Captain Nordheim of the Destroyer Campbell. He begins: "The fanatical suicide attack which caused the death of your son . . ."

(Charlie, downstage, continuing the cable from memory now as Zaretsky continues reading, inaudibly, on the stairs behind him.)

Charlie: ". . . is tragically consistent with the desperate actions of our enemy at this time of their imminent surrender. On the morning of August Sixth a force of eight Zeros descended upon the St. Louis and the Campbell at one-minute intervals; the Sixth and Seventh of these craft being destroyed by Petty Officer Ross from his Forward Forty-Millimeter position, the Eighth now aimed directly for his battle-station. With ample time to leave his position for safety, your son, to his undying honor, remained at his weapon, as determined to destroy the target as was the target to destroy his battle-station. As recommended and re-

viewed by myself and the Secretary of the Navy, it has
been deemed appropriate to recognize his selfless valor
by awarding the Navy Cross to Petty Officer Second-
Class Joseph Ross. In addition, I have respected your
son's prior request to be buried at sea, the Kaddish
being read by an Ensign Sidney Berman for the
name of Jussel Solomon Goldberg, also by the same
request."

*(Starting with the first line of the above speech, the ac-
tion will begin to move forward in time behind Charlie
to the evening of the next day, the first of the seven days
of Shiva, the family's mourning period—daylight giving way to night outside and near-darkness in the bar
as Charlie speaks, Zaretsky slowly folding the cable,
putting on a yarmulkeh, and then joining Young Charlie behind the bar where they drape a large piece of
black cloth over the long bar-mirror; their movements
—and those of the others during this transition—are
deliberate, trancelike, ritualized, as though to the beat
of inaudible music. During the draping of the mirror,
Gusta will have entered from the Apartment, her head
covered with a dark shawl, carrying a tray of pastries
and Eddie's black suit-jacket; she places the tray on the
center table, drapes the jacket over a chair next to it,
then places a piece of black cloth over Joey's Navy photograph above the Jukebox as Eddie, who has remained
quite still at center, slowly puts on his jacket, then sits
at center table, blankly, looking off, as though in a
dream. Young Charlie comes up behind Eddie, delicately places a yarmulkeh on his father's head and then
one on his own as Nick, Hannah, and then Finney come*

quietly through the front door, wearing dark clothes, each bearing a box of pastry, moving slowly, silently, through the half-light of the bar-room; Gusta embracing Hannah, the two women holding onto each other for a few moments before Nick leads Hannah gently away to their table and Gusta sits at the center table near Eddie. After saying the last few words of the memorized Nordheim cable, Charlie pauses a moment, then turns to look at Eddie who remains quite frozen, listless, on his chair. Hannah and Nick at their usual table now, holding hands, Finney in the shadows of his booth, his head bowed. Charlie moves close to Young Charlie and Zaretsky now; having lit the seven-day memorial candle and placed it on the far left table, the old man and the boy sit near its glow, leaning towards each other in quiet conversation.)

Charlie: I'd never said the Mourner's Kaddish before; I knew what the Hebrew words meant—but suddenly that morning in the synagogue it made no sense to me; here in this ancient, ancient prayer for the dead was not a reference, not a phrase . . . not a word about death.

Zaretsky *(leans towards Young Charlie, answering his question)*: It's not *about* death, Chaim; we have here a prayer about faith only, absolute faith in God and his wisdom. *(Closes his eyes.)* Listen, the music of it, "Yisgaddal v'yiskaddash shmey rabboh . . ." You praise God, "B'rich Hu": "blessed be He; blessed, praised, glorified, exalted . . ."

Eddie (*quietly, almost to himself, still looking off*): It's like the Mafia, Charlie . . . It's like talkin' to a Mafia Chief after he does a hit, ya kiss the Capo's ass so he don't knock *you* off too: "Hey, God, what a great idea, killin' Joey Ross. Throwin' my cousin Sunny under a garbage truck—I thought *that* was great—but havin' some nutso Nip drop Joey, this is you at the top of your *form*, baby . . ." (*Gusta rises slowly, staring down at him.*) Oh, yeah, magnified and sanctified be *you*, Don Giuseppe . . . (*Gusta turns sharply, walks quickly to the stairs and exits into the Apartment; Eddie barely glancing at her, continuing louder now, all in bar turning to him.*) Hey, Charlie, that's *it* for Hebrew School. Over and *out*, kid. I hear ya go *near* the goddamn place I bust ya in the chops . . . (*Rises, pulls off his yarmulkeh, then yanks off Young Charlie's.*) *Hell* with the Bar Mitzvah; I'm takin' ya to Norfolk Street and gettin' ya *laid* that day . . . (*As Eddie continues, louder, his rage growing, we begin to hear Gusta singing the old Yiddish lullaby we heard in Act One, distantly, gently, from upstairs.*)

Gusta's Voice (*singing*):
"Oif'n pripitchok,
Brent a faierel,
Un in shtub iz heys . . ."
                    (*Continuing softly through the scene . . .*)

Eddie: . . . Three years Joey put in, the prayers, the bullshit, the Bar Mitzvah shot, the goddamn criminal *con* of the whole thing. I *knew* it—(*Shouting, striding fiercely to bar, tearing black cloth off of mirror.*) I *told* ya, I knew it all *along* it was a sucker's game! You *watch* me, alla you, *tonight* I go to Beth-*El*, I go to the *East Window* because this is where God's supposed t'hear ya better—and I tell 'im, I tell the Killer Bastard—get *this*, God, I ain't a *Jew* no more! *Over*, pal! Fifty years of bein' a Jew Loser; *over*, baby! *Take* 'em, take the *resta* them, they're *yours*—*you* chose 'em, *you* got 'em—

Young Charlie *(quietly)*: Shut up . . .

Eddie: —every *God*-fearin', *death*-fearin', scared-*shit*less *Jew*-creep is *yours*—but not *Eddie*, not—

Young Charlie: Shut up, will ya? *(He rises.)* You really gonna blame this on *God*, Pop? Really? This is what you *wanted*, Pop: Mr. America, the toughest Jew in the Navy, and you got it; only he's dead. Every *letter, twice* on the phone with him I heard ya—"Kill, kill, *kill* 'em, kid!" Same as you screamed in the *ring*. And you want *God* to take the blame for this? *(Pointing fiercely, tears in his eyes.)* All for *you*, Pop, the Ring, the Twin-Forties, he was fightin' for *you*. "Kill 'em, kid! *Get* 'em!" No, Pop, no, not *God*, not *God*—you, it was *you*, it was *you*, Pop. *(He races quickly up the stairs, crying, exits into Apartment, slamming the door behind him.)*

(Silence for a moment, even Gusta's distant singing has stopped. Eddie goes quickly up the stairs to the door.)

Eddie: Listen to me, kid; ya got it all wrong, I straighten it out for ya . . . *(He tries to open the door,*

*but it has clearly been locked from the inside; he leans
closer, raises his voice a bit, trying to talk to Young
Charlie through the door.)* Listen to me, Charlie; it's
just my wacky Pop, see. Just my wacky Pop all over
again. *Fine* points; it's the goddamn *fine* points, kid—
(Louder, almost cracking, his rage holds him together.)
He *knows* this Nip Fruitcake is comin' right *for* 'im,
but he stays there behind his gun, because he *thinks*
he's *supposed* to! It's my Pop all over again, pal—*fine*
points; goddamn fine points! Wacky, the *both* o' them
. . . *wacky . . . (Silence. He tries the knob again.)* Come
on, kid; open up. *(One bang on the door; sternly,
evenly:)* Hey, Charlie; open up. *(Silence.)* Let's move
it, Charlie; let me in. *(Starts banging more forcefully
on door.)* Let me in, Charlie; let me *in* there . . .
*(Now wildly, fiercely, pleading, pounding with all his
strength, the door shaking from his blows.)* Charlie,
Charlie, let me *in*, let me *in*! *(Both fists together now,
pounding rhythmically, shouting with each blow.)* Let
me *in*, let me *in*, let me *in* . . .

*(He continues banging on the door, his shouting almost
like a chant now; Nick and Finney rise as though to
come to his aid; Zaretsky remains on his wooden box,
his head bowed, intoning loudly above the din.)*

Zaretsky: "Yisgaddal v'yiskaddash shmey rabboh . . ."

*(A sudden silence, a sharp drop in light, they are all
quite still, frozen silhouettes in the dim remaining
glow; Charlie alone in a small spotlight at right,
caught by the moment.)*

Charlie *(turns to us; softly, a plea)*: I didn't mean it, I just . . . I mean, I was *twelve* at the time, very upset, a *kid* . . . I was just . . . ya know what I mean?

(The sudden sound of Lyndon Johnson's Voice fills the stage, his echoing drawl offering the promise of the Great Society as Eddie, Zaretsky, Hannah, Nick and Finney exit into the shadows of the bar, the Flamingo Chandelier rising into the darkness above it, Charlie moving slowly down center as this part of his past disappears behind him.)

Johnson's Voice: Is our world gone? We say farewell. Is a new world coming? We welcome it. And we bend it to the hopes of Man . . .

Charlie *(turns to us, brightening)*: Amazingly . . . amazingly, life went back to normal after Joey died— Pop quickly resumed living at the top of his voice and the edge of his nerves, battling with Zaretsky in the mornings and me in the afternoons and re-naming the bar "Big Ed's Club Canal." My next bout with Pop— oh, there were a few minor exhibition matches about leaving home at seventeen, not going to Law School, not visiting often enough—but our next *real* bout was more than twenty years later. October Fifteenth, Sixty-Five; I remember exactly because it was the morning the Vatican Council announced that the Jews were no longer responsible for the death of Christ . . . *(As he continues, an older Gusta, her raven hair streaked with gray, enters from the Kitchen in the dim half-light behind him, carrying a tray; she will move* *briskly from table to table as he speaks, clearing away the many plastic pineapples and coconut shells, eventually disappearing back into the Kitchen.)* By then I had become one of the blue-moon Luftmenshen who had *made* it in the Narrishkeit business. This, starting at the age of twenty-*three*, by knockin' out almost one novel a year. The most familiar to you, from the early Sixties, would be "Over at Izzy's Place," the first of the "Izzy" books, eight and still counting, three best-sellers by then, vast areas of virgin forest consumed by paperback sales, undisputed Middleweight Champ at thirty-four, I had become . . . unavoidable. And so had Izzy. Izzy, tough but warm, blunt yet wise, the impossible and eccentric Bleecker Street tavern-keeper who won not only your heart in the final chapter, but the Mayor's Special Cultural Award that year for "embodying the essential charm and excitement of New York's ethnic street life." *(Shakes his head, smiling.)* Unavoidable, that is, to everyone but Pop. Hard to take it personally, he never read anything longer than Winchell's column or the Blow-by-Blows in the Trib. We were down to maybe four or five visits a year by then—the first half of each being consumed with how long it'd been since the last one and the second half with contractual arrangements for the next—and we didn't meet at the usual family weddings and Bar Mitzvahs because Pop would never again enter a synagogue or any place that resembled one . . . *(Lights coming up slowly on the bar as he continues; Gusta, who has returned from the Kitchen, sits alone now at the center table, business-like, in charge, wearing glasses, checking a stack of bills, as Charlie moves about her in the*

*empty bar-room indicating the places where The Reg-
ulars once sat.)* Hannah was gone by then, and Nick
too; I never did learn their last names. Finney—old,
but sharp as ever—smelled O.T.B. and Legal Lottery
in the wind and was now taking Temperature-Humid-
ity Index bets at a Kosher Delicatessen in Boca Raton.
Mr. Zaretsky died in January of Sixty-One, just a week
before his ninety-third birthday, during the closing
moments of a concert for the Y.M.H.A. of St. Louis, in
Missouri, performing his twelve-minute version of
"The Dybbuk"; passing away in crimson light, playing
all parts . . . including title role. *(Moving down behind
Gusta's chair as she continues busily checking bills.)* I
called Mom every Sunday to hear her two jokes of the
week, but this last call was different—Pop'd had a
mild heart attack in Sixty-Four from which he'd
quickly recovered, but now she said something had
"gone wrong with the health"; I asked for more details
but she was already into her second joke by then—
*(Sound of Eddie laughing loudly from the Kitchen as
though at what Charlie has just said; morning light
starts to stream in from outside as Gusta rises with
her stack of bills, exits briskly up the stairs into
Apartment.)*—so I came down early the next morning
to check it out myself, and found him, as always, in
better shape than *I* was . . . *(Eddie enters from the
Kitchen chuckling happily at something on the front
page of "The New York World-Telegram"; Eddie,
though twenty years older, seems spry enough as he
walks down towards the far right booth, sharply opening the paper to read the rest of the front-page story
that amuses him so much; the front page faces us now*

and we see a huge banner headline which states: "Vatican Absolves Jews Of Crucifixion Blame." Charlie turns to him.) Pop . . .

Eddie *(glances up from paper, pleasantly)*: Hey . . . it's him. *(Returns to paper.)* How ya doin', kid?

Charlie: Fine, fine; I'm—

Eddie: How'd ya get in?

Charlie: I got my key. Listen, Pop, I was . . . uh . . . in the neighborhood, stopped by . . .

Eddie *(sits in booth, still reading paper)*: In the neighborhood?

Charlie: Yeah, right . . . *(Approaches booth, indicating headline.)* Well, I see you've gotten the big news, Pop.

Eddie: Winchell had it two days ago. Just sent the Pope off a telegram on the matter; here's a copy. *(Hands him piece of note paper.)*

Charlie: *(reading)*: I don't think they just hand telegrams to the Pope directly, Pop; especially ones that say, "Thanks a lot, you Greaseball Putz."

Eddie: Well, let's see, must be what?—four, five months now since you last—

Charlie: Let's skip that one this time, O.K.? Mom tells me we got a health problem here.

Eddie *(slaps table, laughing)*: I don't believe it. I don't *believe* it. Six *months* ago I say I'm not feelin' so good, she decides to hear it *now*. That listening thing she does—I'm tellin' ya, kid, it's wackier than ever—the woman hears less and less every week and what she *does* get comes to her entirely by *carrier*-pigeon. *(Charlie smiles; Eddie rises from booth.)* Old news, kid, I'm fine now; looka me. *(Demonstrates a boxing combination.)* Looka me, huh? Also the place is a hit, Charlie; just happened the last few months. Hey, not *giant*, but a hit. *(Chuckles, pointing upstairs.)* *She* did it; the Wacky One. Turns out, right near here, starts out a whole new neighborhood, "HoHo"—

Charlie: That's "SoHo"—

Eddie *(with a sly wink)*: I'm tellin' ya, kid, *Ho*Ho— wall-to-wall Luftmensh, blocks and *blocks* of 'em, doin' nothin' but Narrishkeit, and they got these *galleries* here, hustlin' the Narr for 'em; *bucks*, Charlie, bucks like ya wouldn't believe—and all from this Narrishkeit done by these Luftmensh livin' in these Lufts around here.

Charlie: Lofts, Pop.

Eddie: And the *rent* for these Lufts—I'm talkin' *Vegas* money, Charlie. Anyways, maybe five months ago, a coupla these Narrishkeit Hustlers come in here, they're havin' some o' the Mulligan Stew—they go *crazy* for it—

Charlie: I don't blame them—

Eddie: Next thing I know we got a goddamn *army* o' these Narrishkeit people with the fancy Lufts comin' here, they're gobblin' up everything in sight, they love the stuff and they love Mama—under the original *names*, the Varnishkes, the Holishkes—they come in strangers, they go out grandchildren. I put up a new sign outside, musta seen it, "The Homeland"—I up the prices a little, we're a *hit*; not a cha*malia*, but we're doin' O.K. Your Mom done it. *(Sits at center table.)*

Charlie: She mentioned something about hiring a waitress, but I had no idea—*(sits opposite him)* this is *great*, Pop.

Eddie: Yeah; so how *you* doin'?

Charlie: Well, I'm workin' on a new—

Eddie: Hey, I seen ya on the T.V. last week.

Charlie: Oh?

Eddie: Yeah, you was gettin' some prize for somethin', the Mayor was there.

Charlie: Right.

Eddie: Yeah, I seen ya on the T.V. You come in old.

Charlie: Old?

Eddie: Yeah; I mean, you're a young fellah, but on T.V. you come in old.

Charlie: Pop, do you happen to recall *which* prize it was and *what* I got it for?

Eddie: It was one o' them "Dizzy" books.

Charlie: "Izzy," Pop, "*Izzy*"—

Eddie: Maybe it was the tuxedo.

Charlie: The tuxedo?

Eddie: That made you come in old. Yeah, that's what it was.

Charlie: O.K., Pop, I'm glad you're feeling well, and I'm delighted about the place. *(Rising to leave.)* Now I gotta—

Eddie: O.K.; give my regards to . . . to . . . uh . . .

Charlie: Allison.

Eddie: What happened to Sally?

Charlie: We were divorced three years ago. As you well know.

Eddie *(hits his head)*: Of course. Of course. Hard to keep track, alla them—

Charlie: Pop, I've only been married twice, Sally and *Karen*—

Eddie: Better catch up; that puts you two behind Rita Hayworth. So what's with this . . . uh . . . ?

Charlie: Allison. You've had dinner with her twice. Last time for three hours. She told you she was editing a book that proved Roosevelt did nothing for the Jews during the War. You broke two plates and walked out. She thought you were cute.

Eddie *(after a moment)*: Shit, *marry* that one.

Charlie *(starts towards door)*: O.K., I really gotta—

Eddie: Right; hugs to Sarah and Josh—hey, Josh; where's my Josh? Been a coupla *months* now—

Charlie: He was hanging around here entirely too much, Pop, it was—

Eddie: We talk things *over*, we *discuss* things—

Charlie: Pop, he's the only ten-year-old at Dalton who drinks his milk out of a shot-glass.

Eddie (*laughs happily*): A *pisser*, that kid; goddamn *pisser*—

Charlie (*opens door*): Right; see ya around—

Eddie (*quietly*): O.K., them books, I read one. (*Charlie turns at door, his hand on knob.*) Well, not *read*; I give it a skim. The first one. (*Chuckling.*) That's some *sweet*heart, that guy. Who *is* that guy? The bartender with the two sons, comes from Russia; who *is* that sweetie? Got *all* sweeties in there, y'sweet blind lady, y'sweet ex-cop, y'sweet bookie—*three* pages, I got an attack o' diabetes.

Charlie: Pop, if I told the truth they'd send a *lynch*-mob down here for ya.

Eddie: Always glad to see new customers, kid. This guy in the book, supposed to be a Jewish guy, right? What kinda Jew is that? Don't sound like no Jew *I* ever heard. Could be anything—Italian, Irish, some kinda Chink even. (*Turns to newspaper.*) Well, what the hell, regardless, I wanna wish ya good luck with them "Dizzy" books.

Charlie: Izzy! (*Closes door, turns to him.*) Izzy, Izzy, *Izzy*. As you know damn *well*. O.K., that's it. No more, Pop, that was *it*. I am never playing this fucking game again; it's *over*. (*Moving towards him.*) Izzy? You don't like him? Not Jewish enough for ya? He's *your Jew*, Pop, you made him up. He's *your* Jew, and so am I; no history, no memory, the only thing I'm linked to is a chain of bookstores. Vos *vilst* du?—that's Yiddish, Pop; it means "What do you *want*?" God bothered you, we got rid of him. Hugging bothers you, we do not touch. Here I am, Pop, just what the Rabbi ordered; only now you don't like it; now you don't want it. Vos vilst du, Goldberg? *(Leans towards him at table.)* That prize you don't know the *name* of for the books you never *read* —I *won* it, Pop, me, the *air*-person, I *did* it—*(bangs fist on table, shouting)*—right here at this bar, everything you *asked* for. I am an honest-to-God, red-white-and-blue, *American fucking millionaire.* A *mil*, Pop, a *mil*, a *bundle*! And I never sleep, only in moving vehicles, I hail a cab to take a nap; I work, I work, there's like a fire in me and I don't know where it is so I cannot put it out. And the fire is you. I *did* it, Pop. I won. K.O. in the first *round*. Vos *vilst* du, Papa? Vos *vilst* du fun mir? What do you fucking *want*?

(Silence for a moment. Eddie remains quite still.)

Eddie *(quietly)*: You shouldn't use "fuck" in a sentence, Charlie, you never put it in the right place. You don't blow good, kid, never did; ya don't have the knack. Another item: I listen to ya, I don't like the scorin' on this bout. How about *I* get credit for all the hits and *you* get the credit for bein' a nervous nut. *(Rises from chair, his old energy.)* What're you, Goddamn Zorro the Avenger? What? You lookin' to come back here with your empties and get a *re*fund? I didn't *order* this item, you ain't a *cake* I baked. I wasn't just your *Pop*, or Joey's neither, I'm Eddie; for this I take all blame or commendations. Nothin' else. I lived in *my* time, now you gotta live in *yours*, pal, and you can't send me the goddamn bill. Give it *up*, kid, give it the hell *up*. Give yourself a rest, you'll waste your life tryin' to catch me, you'll find y'self twenty years from now runnin' around a cemetery tryin' to put a stake through my heart. Sure I screwed up; now it's *your* turn. Yeah, let's see what *you* do when you look at Sarah or Josh and see *your* Pop's eyes peekin' out at ya; or worse, your *own*. Let's see what ya *do*, kid. *(Turns, starts towards bar.)* Meanwhile, currently, I admit I give ya a hard time— but, frankly, I never liked Rich Kids. *(He stops, stands quite still; speaks briskly:)* O.K., conversation over. End of conversation. See ya around; goodbye—*(Grips back of chair, staggers, as though about to faint, whispering:)* Shit, here we go again . . . *(He suddenly falls to the ground, the chair clattering down with him.)*

Charlie *(rushing to him, breathless)*: Pop, Jesus . . . Pop . . .

Eddie *(almost immediately, sitting up)*: It's O.K., it's O.K., get me a vodka . . .

Charlie *(helping him up)*: Pop, I thought you—

Eddie: *Vodka*, get me a vodka—*(Charlie races behind the bar; Eddie, standing now but still a bit unsteady, leans on the table for a moment.)* O.K., O.K. now. Comes, then it goes. *(Walking slowly to bar.)* Comes, then it goes. Fine now. Perfect. *(Charlie, behind bar, quickly pouring a glass of vodka, handing it out to him—but Eddie grabs the bottle and takes a long swig* *directly from it.)* Excellent. Excellent. *(Sets bottle down on bar, renewed. Silence for a moment.)* O.K., I conned ya, Charlie . . . I got this heart thing; special disease named for some Goy, Smithfield. Your Mother says right off, "How come you got Smithfield's Disease and he don't got yours?" Don't care how old the joke is, what the occasion, she tells it. Turns out that wasn't no heart attack last year, it was this Smithfield number. The valve closes up, you keep fallin' asleep, fallin' over—*(Pulls wheelchair out from behind far end of bar.)* I'm supposed to sit in this thing alot because I keep droppin' alla time. What kills you is these Embies—

Charlie *(quietly)*: I think that's . . . that's Embolus, Pop . . .

Eddie *(moving wheelchair down left)*: Right. Anyways you can shoot off these Embies anytime. They go all over the joint. Musta shot one off four weeks ago, I'm all screwed up, I go in for these tests—turns out I'm the proud owner of a new, fully automatic *Smithfield*. Knocks you off in like six months or maybe next Tuesday. So—*(sits down in wheelchair)* good ya stopped by, we do a wrap-up shot, I got a *job* for ya—

Charlie *(sits next to wheelchair)*: The doctors, they're *sure?*—I mean, I can get you—

Eddie: Minute I get the news I got only one item concerns me, see; I go down to Barney's Tattoo Parlor on Mott, take care of it right off, goddamn relief. Looka here—*(Rolls up both sleeves, Charlie comes closer to look at the two tattoos.)* One says "Pistol Pete," see, nice gun picture there, and this one here—

Charlie *(reading elaborate red and blue tattoo on Eddie's left arm; confused)*: "King Of The Twin-Forties." I don't—

Eddie *(triumphantly)*: Hebrew *law*, Charlie—one of the oldest—you can't get buried in *any* Jewish Cemetery if you got tattoos! Twenty *years*, kid, I ain't had to be no kinda *Jew* at *all*—coulda ended up gettin' *Kaddished*-over, full-out ceremony, then gettin' stuck in some sacred Jew-ground with a buncha Yiddlach for *eternity*! *(Quietly, glancing upstairs:)* She ain't to be trusted on this issue; since Joey, the woman is a goddamn religious *fanatic*—candles, prayers, every weird little holiday—*(Leans towards Charlie, grips his arm.)* So, here's the job, Charlie—*anything* goes wrong, I want your personal guarantee—

Charlie: Of course, Pop—

Eddie *(hands him card from wallet)*: Here's where ya put me, kid; place in Queens, no religions whatever, no Gods of any type.

Charlie: It's done.

Eddie: Because the woman, I'm tellin' ya, she's got her eye on this spot in Brooklyn where they planted the

Actor. Woman thinks dyin' is movin' to the *suburbs*, wants us all *together* there—me, her, Ethel, and *Zaretsky*! Can ya *picture* it, Charlie?—me and Zaretsky, goddamn *room*-mates *forever*! Wouldn't get a minute's rest. 'Specially *now*, what I know *now* . . . *(He looks away. Silence for a moment.)*

Charlie: *What?* What do you know now?

Eddie *(pause; a deep breath, plunges in)*: O.K.—*day* before he goes to St. Louis, the man gets a flash he's gonna kick it, makes out a will. Man is ninety-god-damn-*three*, he's first makin' out a will. Brings a lawyer over here, *also* about a hundred and eight, Ruskin, used to do all his business when he had the New Marinsky on Houston, wants me and Finney to witness, sign the will. I look it over, I see two things—first, I'm not in it; second, whatever he's got is goin' to the State of Israel . . . whatever he's *got* bein' one million, five hundred thousand dollars and change. A mil and a half, Charlie; the man was sittin' on a *mil* and a *half*. And this Ruskin almost as rich; *Ruskin*, with an accent on 'im made Zaretsky sound like George M. *Cohan*! They sell this Marinsky dump for bupkes back in Twenty-Eight; they parlay the bupkes into a fortune, they was good at *business, American business*, and the rest he got from them goddamn *concerts*, Charlie! *(A pause; he rubs the arm of the wheelchair.)* I made Finney promise to zip it; I never told you, Gusta, nobody . . .

Charlie: Hey, far as me and Joey were concerned, you were always the *boss* here; wouldn't've made any difference—

Eddie: A mil and a *half*, Charlie—he's livin' in that little room, takin' shit from me—

Charlie: He *loved* it here, Pop—he even liked fightin' with *you*, he—

(Charlie stops in mid-sentence, aware that Eddie has started to nod off to sleep . . . Eddie suddenly hits the arm of his wheelchair, forcing himself awake.)

Eddie: *(outraged)*: A *millionaire*, Charlie! Workin' in a loser language! He did everything *wrong*—and he was a hit! Can you make *sense* of this, Charlie? *Zaretsky*, why *him*—why *him* and not *me*? And, you'll forgive me—I wish ya all the best—*(gripping Charlie's arm)* but why *you*, ya little Putz, you with your goddamn *Narr*ishkeit—why *you*, and not me? Why? *(Starting to become drowsy again.)* Surrounded by goddamn millionaires here . . . Can you make *sense* of this . . . the Bucks, what happened? The Big Bucks, why did they avoid me? Wherever I was, the Bucks never came, and when I went to where the Bucks were they flew away like pigeons . . . like pigeons in the park . . . *(His head nodding forward, drifting off.)* Got this dream alla time I'm at Ellis Island, only I'm the age I'm now. Old days, you had a disease, they wouldn't let ya in. They mark on your coat with chalk, "E" for eye, "L" for lung, and they send ya back. In the dream, I got an "H" for heart and they won't let me in . . . they won't let me in, Joey . . . *(He falls deeply asleep in the wheelchair. Silence. Charlie leans anxiously towards him.)*

Charlie: Pop . . . ? *(Touches his arm gently.)* Pop . . . ? *(Silence again. Charlie rises, carefully turning the wheelchair around so that Eddie's sleep is not disturbed by the morning light that comes in from the front door. Eddie remains with his back to us; during this next scene we will not see his face except perhaps for brief glimpses of his profile. Charlie speaking to us as he turns the chair.)* Six weeks later one o' them Embies shot off into the left side of Pop's brain, paralyzing his right arm and leg and taking away his ability to speak. *(Opening small side table on arm of wheelchair, placing pad and pencil on it.)* Two weeks back from the hospital he had somehow taught himself to write almost legibly with his left hand—according to this terrific Speech Therapy lady I went to, this meant he could eventually be trained to speak again. But all he was able to produce were these unintelligible, childlike noises, and he refused to see anyone, no less try to *speak* to anyone, including Gusta. He closed "The Homeland" down and sat here. Ten days, like this. On the eleventh day, armed with some hints from the Speech Therapist, I came down to take a shot. *(To Eddie:)* Delighted to see me, huh? *(Eddie shakes his head angrily.)* And you're thinkin' what's the sense of trying to learn how to speak again because you figure you *can't*, also why torture yourself if you ain't gonna live that much longer *anyway*, right? *(Eddie points with his left hand as though to say "You got it," then* *does a powerful "Go away" gesture.)* Right. And there's these clear pictures in your head of all the words you want to say and your mouth just won't do the job, right? *(Eddie does not respond. Then, after a moment, he nods "Yes.")* O.K., now I don't know *how* this works or *why* this works, but there's a thing you're capable of right now called "Automatic Speech." As impossible as it must feel to you, you are capable, right now, of saying, distinctly as *ever*, certain automatic phrases— ends of songs, if I do the first part, a piece of a prayer, something. And, thing is, you hear yourself *do* that and that'll get you to want to work at the whole talkin'- shot again, see. *(Eddie scribbles something on the pad on the arm of his wheelchair, hands pad to Charlie.)* "Go *away*. *Stay* away." Pop, I gotta try the number here. C'mon, gimme a chance . . . *(Charlie leans forward, singing softly:)* "Oh beautiful for spacious skies . . ." *(Pause, no response. Charlie tries again.)* "Oh beautiful for spacious skies, for amber . . ." *(Silence for a few moments; then very suddenly, sharply:)* You got some ice-cold Daitch on tap, fellah?

Eddie *(suddenly)*: I got it, now *you* . . . got it. *(Eddie realizes what he has just done. Charlie smiles. Silence for a moment; Eddie appears to be chuckling softly.)*

Charlie: Well, now. Shall we proceed, sir? *(Silence for a moment. Eddie turns away; then looks at Charlie; he nods.)* O.K., now we got some pictures here . . . *(Takes a stack of eight-by-eleven-inch cards out of an envelope.)* Objects, people, animals, O.K.? Double item here, see; there's a picture of the thing and then the word for it printed underneath. You go for either one —word or picture, and *say* what it is. Be patient with yourself on this, O.K.? *(Eddie nods.)* O.K.; animals and birds. *(Looks through cards, stops at one; smiles.)* Yeah, here's a good beginning . . . *(He turns the card around; it is a full-color illustration of a duck.)* "Duck." We'll start with "Duck."

(Eddie does not move, there is a long silence. Then Eddie, rather forcefully, raises his left arm, the middle finger of his hand jabbing upward, giving Charlie "The Finger." Eddie continues to hold his hand up firmly; the lights come down, one single light remaining on "The Finger."

Charlie *(turns to us)*: Well, there it is, my last image of my father: his memorial, his obelisk, his Washington Monument. *(He moves across towards his booth at far right, the light gradually dimming down on "The Finger" during his next speech; only a small spotlight on Charlie, the rest of the stage in near-darkness.)* He died about seven months later; by then he was talking, even hollering, and terrorizing his third Speech Therapist. *(We hear the distant sound of a Cantor singing a phrase of the Kaddish, rising then fading, as the barely visible shape of the older Gusta comes out of the Kitchen; she rolls the wheelchair off into the shadows as Charlie continues.)* Bicentennial's next week, two hundred years since America was born and, two days later, ten years since Pop died. I wish I could tell you that he won my heart in the final chapter, but he did not. I light his Yahrzeit candle every year, though, and say the prayer; I figured Mom would appreciate it. *(After a moment.)* It's a month now since *she* died, joking as she closed her act. "I'm thinking of becoming a Catholic," she says, that last night. "And why's that, Ma?" I say, feeding her the straight-line like a good son—*(With Gusta's accent:)* "Well, Sonny, I figure better one of *them* goes than one of us." *(Takes keys from jacket.)* I miss her, of course; but I will not miss this place. *(A beat.)* Pop got his wish, of course; I buried him in this aggressively non-sectarian joint called Hamilton Oaks out in Queens. However, one of the reasons I never forget his Yahrzeit is that every year, a week before the Sixth . . . *(he takes the familiar blue and white card out of his jacket)* this card comes from the Sons of Moses to remind me. For fifty bucks he got them to find me for the *rest of my life*. Los Angeles, *London*, the Virgin fucking *Islands*, they *find* me, those Sons of Moses . . .

(The sudden lights of the Present—the early evening light of the beginning of the play—come up in the barroom as Charlie holds the card up and crushes it fiercely in his hand; he tosses the mangled card on the floor and strides angrily towards the bar, the old Stroller once again down left, his rage building as he slams noisily about behind the bar looking for his glass and vodka bottle.)

Charlie: The old switcheroo—the old switcheroo every time! Never made any *sense, never*—his *head*, his *head*, it was *Steeple*chase up there, the goddamn *Roller*-coaster—*(Bangs his fist on the bar.)* None* of it, nothing he said, *none* of it fit together—*none* of it—*still* doesn't—son of a bitch—

Josh *(entering briskly from the Apartment above, carrying two cartons; brightly)*: Dad . . . Dad, I've been thinking, how about—why don't we *keep* this place and just get somebody to *run* it for us; y'know, a manager, we'll find a good manager. We *keep* it, Dad, we keep it just the way it *is*; I'll help out, weekends, every summer, maybe even—

Charlie *(fiercely, wildly, shouting)*: I *told* you, we're *selling* it, we're selling it, you don't *listen*—

Josh *(startled)*: I just—I just thought maybe we could—

Charlie *(he smashes his fist on the bar, coming quickly out from behind bar towards Josh)*: It's *gone, over*, outa *my* life, outa *yours, over, over*—(Charlie, blindly, violently, his fist raised, advancing on Josh, Josh backing fearfully away across the room)—you don't *listen*, you *never did*—you don't *now*, you never *did*, and you never *will*—

(Josh is trapped against one of the booths, startled, frozen. Charlie stops, stands quite still, trembling with his own rage; then gradually begins to focus on his son's frightened eyes.)

Charlie *(lost, whispering)*: Josh . . . sorry, I was . . .

(Josh backs away towards the front door, warily, as though from a stranger.)

Josh *(softly)*: You get yourself together, O.K. . . . ? I'll wait in the car, O.K. . . . ?

Charlie: Josh, I'm sorry . . . I was . . . see, I was . . .

Josh: You get yourself together, I'll be in the car . . .

Charlie *(moving towards him, his hand up)*: Josh, what happened, let me explain . . .

(But Josh has gone out into the street with his cartons, the door closing behind him. Charlie stands exhausted at the center of the room, looking at the door; silence for several moments. He turns, looks about at the bar for a moment, sees the crumpled Sons of Moses card on the floor; he picks it up, studies it thoughtfully, then starts straightening it out as he walks slowly towards the bar. We begin to hear the violin introduction to Aaron Lebedeff's recording of "Rumania" from the Jukebox, and then Lebedeff's rousing voice.)

Lebedeff's Voice:
   "Rumania, Rumania, Rumania . . .
   Geven amol a land a zise, a sheyne . . ."

(As Charlie reaches the bar and sits on one of the stools, the old bar-lights fade quickly up, the colorful lights of the Thirties and Forties, and Eddie enters briskly from the Kitchen, the younger Eddie with his fine white

*shirt, black bow-tie and sharp black pants; Eddie goes
directly behind the bar, takes a glass and a bottle from
the shelf, pours with his usual flourish and sets a drink
down next to Charlie; Charlie looking down at the card
as the Lebedeff Music fills the room, Eddie leaning forward with his hands on the bar, looking at the front
door, waiting for customers, as . . .)*

THE CURTAIN FALLS

About the Author

Herb Gardner is the author of *A Thousand Clowns, The Goodbye People, Thieves, I'm Not Rappaport* (which won the 1986 Tony Award for Best Play, the Outer Critics Circle Award for Outstanding Play, and the John Gassner Playwriting Award), and *Conversations With My Father*. His one-act plays include *How I Crossed the Street for the First Time All by Myself, The Forever Game*, and *I'm With Ya, Duke*. For his film adaptation of his play *A Thousand Clowns*, Mr. Gardner won the Best Screenplay Award from the Screenwriters Guild as well as Academy Award nominations for Best Screenplay and Best Picture of the Year. He also wrote the screenplays for *Thieves, The Goodbye People* (which he also directed), and *Who Is Harry Kellerman and Why Is He Saying Those Terrible Things About Me?*—this last being an adaptation of one of his several short stories, which appeared in *The Best American Short Stories of 1968*. In addition, Mr. Gardner is the author of a novel, *A Piece of The Action*. He is currently adapting his award-winning play *I'm Not Rappaport* for the screen.